TANGO TERROIR
a happy feeling that is danced

AUGUSTO TOMAS

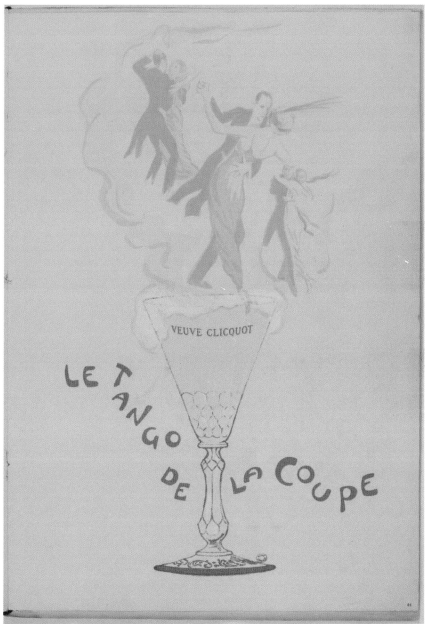

Figure 1: Album Tangoville-sur-mer : Le Tango de la Coupe, 1913, illustration by Sem (aka Georges Goursat)

DEDICATION

I dedicate this book to my daughter Beatriz

Figure 2: "Tango de Salón", illustration by Daniel de Losques, magazine Femina, Paris, 1913 October 15

CONTENTS

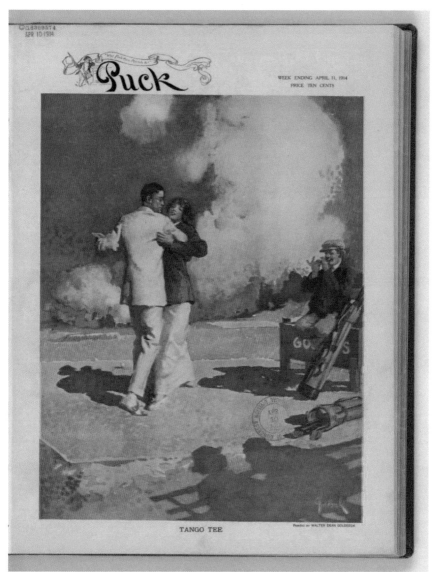

Figure 3: "Tango Tee", illustration painted by Walter Dean Goldbeck in 1914. Illustration shows a man and a woman dancing on the tee at a golf course while the caddy plays the harmonica, cover of magazine Puck, New York, 1914 April 11

1 THE TANGO QUEST

Terroir (/tɛˈrwɑːr/, French: [tɛʁwaʁ]; from terre, "land") is a French term used to describe the environmental factors that affect a crop's phenotype, including unique environment contexts, farming practices and a crop's specific growth habitat. Collectively, these contextual characteristics are said to have a character; Terroir also refers to the Tango's character.

In 1913, the French poet Jean Richepin made a famous speech in honor to the Tango at the most important Academie Française:

I. About the Tango – by Jean Richepin, 1913
II. The Historic "Tango" – newspapers articles, 1913
III. The Possessed of the Tango – by Georges Goursat, 1912
IV. The Tango in Paris – by Carlos Pereyra, 1913
V. The Tango in Buenos Aires – by Enrique Carrillo, 1914

I. About the Tango – by Jean Richepin, 1913

À propos du Tango
Le 25 octobre 1913
Jean RICHEPIN
DISCOURS
DE
M. Jean RICHEPIN
Délégué de l'Académie française
PRONONCÉ DANS LA SÉANCE PUBLIQUE ANNUELLE
DES CINQ ACADÉMIES
Le Samedi 25 octobre 1913
https://www.academie-francaise.fr/propos-du-tango

About the Tango

Gentlemen,

In order to calm certain astonishments, pushed to the point of bewilderment sometimes, even to the point of indignation, to respond to some severe censors more royalist than the king and reminding us of gravity on the simple announcement of the reading that I was going to have the honour to tell you, allow me first of all to affirm how much the subject of this reading, despite appearances to the contrary, not only has nothing unfortunate about it which risks swallowing up your benevolent attention, but is also rather to be one of the best suited to solicit it, to retain it, to be an interesting and rich subject for reflection of all kinds, and that it is worthy of being submitted to you without fearing a futile use of your precious leisure, and that each of you is prepared by his special studies to bring us invaluable insights into it, and that thus, in short (why should I not have the audacity to state my whole thought?) the only competent audience before which we can and we must talk r as befits the Tango, it is, essentially, a plenary session bringing together the five classes of the Institute.

The only point on which one would conceive some doubt is to know which class, among the five, is best in a position to be passionate about such a subject and to provide, for the various problems it suggests, the most important solutions.

And no doubt, at first glance, it seems natural to decide that this privileged class is the Academy of Fine Arts, which unquestionably falls under Dance, including Tango. And it goes without saying that, if we stick to the only technique, the present reading calls for, not my humble voice of a layman, but the authorized voice of a colleague belonging to this class which governs the Arts in general, and, therefore, the dance in particular, and consequently, even more in particular, the Tango. And here, suddenly, obliged to take my place, the eminent colleague who was formerly director of the Fine Arts, and who is today perpetual secretary of the Academy of Fine Arts, my friend Henry Roujon.

But he himself, I am sure, would hasten to say that technique alone does not constitute the whole of an art, and that, in order to discuss it more broadly and at the same time more amiably, one must also think of what its history is, scholarly or anecdotal, and, even more, what is its philosophy, ideal, soul.

And immediately, see with what eagerness would come to the rescue, to drive me out of my usurped function, the other classes of the Institute, having just in their intimate attributions the guard and the worship of its venerable domains, where I have no right to hunt, but look like poaching, especially history and philosophy.

What exquisite and unforeseen things, moreover, would teach us then, although having probably never thought about it much, but suddenly applying their erudition to the inexhaustible treasures, the Academy of Inscriptions and Belles-Lettres and the Academy of Moral and Political Sciences.

Just in the dim light provided by my simple memories of a humanist, I glimpse fabulous palaces opening up their wonders to us. I contemplate there, reviving, all the past life of Dance since its sacred origins; since the times when it was religious, invented and practiced by the gods to symbolize in the eyes of mortals the creation of the world, the circle of the stars in the firmament; since the days when ancient Greece, this youth of humanity, formulated there the teaching of Beauty and the eurythmy of the soul flourishing by the eurythmy of the body.

I remember that Zeus, Demeter, Apollo, were described as dancers by my great ancestor Pindar, that the fierce Artemis also loved to dance, and even the austere Pallas Athenaeum, and that the first choirs of dancing men and women were organized by my other ancestor, even greater than Pindar, and almost a god, the poet, musician and dancer Orpheus!

And I remember, likewise, my Cornelius Nepos, congratulating the Theban hero Epaminondas on having excelled in the dance; and of Homer, showing me among the Phaeacians, before Odysseus delighted with joy, the young men dancing while the bard Demodokos sings; and of Plato, in his Laws, demanding dancing as the crowning achievement of a good education; and of old Socrates, ashamed of not knowing the dance, and, in an attempt to be a complete sage, having lessons in it from Aspasia; and of Sophocles, finally, designated as the most beautiful ephebe of his time and celebrating, by his dance in front of the Athenian people, the victory of our civilization over barbarism, the immortal Salamis!

And may other beautiful things still dance in my memory! And that others, and endless others, could tell us, no longer as a poet who sows them in flight, but as scholars, with supporting documents, our colleagues from the

Academy of Moral Sciences and policies! And in a way, fear not, entertaining! For good French erudition, which knows just as much and more often more than such and such a rogue and important air, also knows the art of saying it with grace, what it knows; and the index cards between the fingers become flowers that you put in the corner of your lips.

So she would reveal to you charming secrets about the Tango in person, do not doubt it! How could she not tell you, since I myself have some, me, poor Gautier-without-knowing about Science? But yes, on the Tango known to the Ancients! Know, in fact, that in the British Museum, one can see, coming from the hypogea of Thebes, dancers who dance it, having for only clothing a belt in braid of gold threads. And also know that it is spoken of in Claudian, a Parnassian long before the letter, the José-Maria de Heredia of the 4th century. And know, moreover, that even before this time, Martial also mentions it in some of his epigrams:

Edere lascivos ad Boetica crusmata gestus
Ed Gaditanos ludere docta modos.

He goes so far as to teach us that then, as now, there were Tango teachers, sent by Cadiz, as ours are sent by the new American Cadiz.

And of Gadibus improbus magister.

And if, were it while running and by chance of memory, I can quote you, in connection with the Tango, similar details, think, once again, of all that a true erudite, belonging to the Academy of Registrations and Belles-Lettres or at the Academy of Moral and Political Sciences!

Not to mention the philosophical exegesis which it would have the right, and the duty, to talk to you about! Because there is a Metaphysics and a Mystique of the dance. Would there therefore also be a Metaphysics and a Mystique of Tango I dare not say. But why wouldn't there be? There is indeed, and this undeniably, deign to think about it, a Mathematics of Tango.

And here is what brings me back, repentant and very humble, to that of the five classes of the Institute that I almost forgot, and to which I offer my full apologies, and which is undoubtedly the most serious of the five, and which by that very fact seems to be the farthest from Tango, and which nevertheless would have to reveal to us the strangest and most disturbing mysteries, since, by its Mathematics, Tango belongs to the Academy of Sciences. Who knows if she would not teach us by $a + b$ that the Tango is the last survival of one of those sacred dances where the Egyptian and Chaldean priests represented the evolutions of the Being and wrote the mathematical formula for the eyes of the Initiates? Who knows if, in the complicated operations of his steps, this mysterious and slow ballet for two does not represent the first blossoming of the Numbers emerging from the creative unity, and which led Pythagoras to give the world the number as its soul, while that the tenebrous Heraclitus concluded that the essence of things is the rhythm of its despairing πάντα ῥεῖ, the eternal flow of everything, with this aggravation provided by Greek grammar, of a neutral subject which is plural while its verb is singular? And who knows finally if the dancers of the Tango, although they know nothing of these formidable things, do not test themselves, however, the obscure and unconscious obsession, and if it is not from there that comes to them the air of application, reflection, absorption, almost sad, sometimes gloomy, brought by some of them to a pleasure which thus seems a kind of morose delight?

Also, we must not dwell too much on these problems which the association of ideas between the Academy of Sciences and Tango has just led us to. It is enough that we have given a glimpse here (very summarily, moreover) of all the varied studies that this poor dance, which some considered unworthy of your attention, could provide to the various classes of the Institute. The little time I have left to speak to you about it, I would like to employ in pleading the cause of this innocent defendant, and I will do so as briefly as possible.

The three great reproaches with which the Tango is overwhelmed have as their causes its foreign origin, its popular origin, and its indecorous character.

There is no need to respond to this last grievance, which is really too unfair, the inappropriateness of a dance being never attributable to the dancers alone. I had the joy of seeing Tangos danced by princesses, and which were models of elegant distinction; and I have seen, on the other hand, formerly, the insipid polka and the honest quadrille of the Lancers danced in such a way, as one of our illustrious predecessors said, to make monkeys blush.

As for the foreign origin of the Tango, it is bizarre that it is incriminated in this hospitable Paris where the English contredanse, the German waltz, the Polish mazurka, the Hungarian polka, the Lithuanian Scottish, the Czech Redowa and American Boston.

Remains the popular origin! And here the detractors of Tango have it easy, it seems, and do not hesitate to abuse it, modestly veiling their faces at the idea that, for him, this skinned, this scabby, popular is not enough to say, and must be pronounced pejoratively "popular". So, think! A dance which had for cradles the most disgusting dives of America! A dance of cowherds, grooms, gauchos, half-savages, negroes! the horror!

– Ah! sigh these fierce moralists, let us restore the pretty and delicate dances of our ancestors, the dances in which the delicacy and grace of the French aristocracy flourished exquisitely!

They flourish in the same way, gentlemen the fierce moralists, in the

Tango, in this Tango resulting from the worst dens, when it is danced as I told you earlier. And for the rest, learn this, since you don't know it, namely that those famous dances of yesteryear, those aristocratic dances of our ancestors, so pretty, so fine, so delicate, so graceful, all also began by being dances popular. All, yes, all are of rustic birth; all are old peasant branles, old sarcasms invented by villains, all down to the suave minuet, first round country poitevin, up to the haughty and charming gavotte, made fashionable by Queen Marie-Antoinette, and whose first cadences were punctuated by the clicks of the big hooves shoed by the heavy guys from Brittany.

Because they have always loved dancing, our peasants and the Auvergne and Bourbon bourrée proves that they still love it both in the fields and in the ballrooms of the Parisian suburbs, the bourrée, perhaps more complicated than the Tango. And, like our peasants, our people of the world also love dancing; and, if they refine it, once taken from the people, as they are doing now for the Tango, they still leave it its complications, its ardor, its violence, while giving their efforts the elegant turn which suits them. And that is why, in his Orphésographie, the canon of Langres Thoinot-Arbeau, master of the chapel of Henri III, described this exercise, these veritable gymnastics of the Dance, in terms in which you will see all the movements that the Tango synthesizes precisely, although it conceals them under the concentrated ardor of its secret and grave mimicry.

« To dance, writes the good canon, that is to say to jump, saultelotter, carole, baler, treper, trepiner, move and move the feet, hands and bodies of certain cadences, measures and movements consisting of saulz, bends of the body, divarications, claudications, ingeniculations, elevations, jactations of feet and other countenances. »

And, to conclude, what does the foreign and popular origin of a dance really matter? And what does his character and face matter? We francize everything, and the dance we love becomes French. And so, we must see, in the current craze for Tango, only the renewal of our tenacious love for dance, and we should rejoice in it. Because France is, like ancient Greece, and alone with it, a country where dance is necessary to life.

When Odysseus arrives at the dreadful isle where Polyphemus and the cannibalistic Cyclopes dwell, and when he asks old Silenus what this land of horror is, Dionysos' foster-father defines it with a single epithet; he calls it ἀχορον χθονα, a land where there is no dancing.

Well! France must never become that land! She can only become one under penalty of death. Let us bless all that prevents it, all that revives the old tradition by which it resurrects ancient Greece, by remaining a land where we dance, where we do while dancing, where we even know how to die dancing.

Isn't this what the Spartans did at Thermopylae, they who, on the morning of their last day, combed their hair, rubbed their bodies with oil and softened their muscles with a pyrrhic? And isn't it in the same spirit that the great Condé, to storm the impregnable Lérida, made his musketeers climb there to the song of the violins of Lulli? And, likewise, were they not of the same lineage, the twenty-five thousand bearded caps of Austerlitz who broke the enemy center to the fifreli of the fifes whistling a rigodon at them?

Ah! Certainly, they loved dancing, and they knew how to dance, all these heroes! And that's why, when I was a child of the troops, we were right to be taught dance together with fencing. And that's why I remembered it, first of all, to dare to speak about the Tango in front of the five classes of the Institute, certain that I would be forgiven for this audacity, since by the Tango I mean the dance, and since the dance evokes the Pyrrhic, this Pyrrhic invented by Pallas Athenaeus the wise, this exalted Pyrric that all the young people of Athens, after the performance of Aeschylus' Persians, began to dance like madmen all night long, through the squares and the streets, and especially in front of the temples where they banged their fists on the shields hanging from the doors, and redoubled their frenzied leaps, crying wildly: « Patrie! Patrie! Patrie! »

Jean Richepin*

*Jean Richepin (4 February 1849 – 12 December 1926) was a French poet, novelist and dramatist. His plays, though occasionally marred by his characteristic propensity for dramatic violence of thought and language, constitute in many respects his best work. Most of these were produced at the Comédie française.

II. The Historic "Tango" – newspapers articles, 1913

THE HISTORIC "TANGO"
New York Times
Paris, October 26
https://paperspast.natlib.govt.nz/newspapers/OAM19131217.2.28
https://paperspast.natlib.govt.nz/newspapers/DOM19131224.2.112

"The Historic "Tango"

The large and peaceful hall of the Instituto of France [Academie Française] was packed with a very select and fashionable crowd yesterday, at the annual gathering of the five academies which form the venerable Institute of France, to hear M. Jean Richepin, the famous poet, lecture on the Tango dance.

The grave members of the academy had made it clear to M. Richepin that it would rather ignore his beloved Tango, when it was known that this would be his subject.

There were indeed very few members of the academy present at the lecture, but M. Richepin had a very "chic" audience.

Fashion able society ladies, the aristocracy, and Paris actresses were present in large numbers.

The lecturer boldly attacked the view that the Tango was not quite a suitable subject.

He declared that the most appropriate audience for such a lecture was a gathering of representatives of the five academies of France.

He disposed of the reproach of the vulgarity of the Tango and asserted that no dance was vulgar unless the dancers made it so.

« I have seen the Tango danced by princesses, — declared M. Richepin — and the steps were models of elegance and distinction.

I have also seen the polka and the lancers danced in a way that would make a monkey blush. »

As to the plebeian origin of the Tango, he asserted that all the graceful dances of the old-time aristocracy came from the peasants.

The dancers of mythology and Ancient Greece were patrons of the Tango, he said.

It was an error to suppose that the Tango was unknown to the ancients, and M. Richepin referred to the fact that in the British Museum could be seen girls dancing in much the same way as was now being witnessed.

There were professors of the Tango in those days sent from Cadiz, just as to-day from the new American academies.

When M. Richepin sat down he was loudly cheered."

"The Dance of the day

Under the lofty, classical dome of the Institute of France, at the annual combined meeting of the five French Academies: Academies of Science, Inscription and Belles-lettres, of Political and Moral Sciences, of Fine Arts, of the Forty Immortals — the tango has actually been discussed and extolled by no less a poet and a personage than Jean Richepin. So, an amazing, an unprecedented occasion. Behold the grave, severe Institute thronged with dim-eyed old sages, keen-faced doctors, famous painters and litterateurs, distinguished philosophers and politicians, elegant worldlings with their inseparable opera glasses, chocolate boxes, chatelaines, and fans — and hear massive and handsome Jean Richepin, in the illustrious green uniform of the Academician, his sword strapped to his side, at once disconcerting and delighting his audience with an eloquent defence of the Dance of the Day.

It has been attacked because sometimes it becomes indecorous. That is the fault of the dancers, not of the dance. « I have seen it performed by princesses — a spectacle of elegance and distinction; but else where I have seen the insipid polka, the honest, mechanical lancers danced in a fashion which, in the words of the younger Damas, would make the monkeys blush."

After this, a torrent of beautifully expressed praise of dancing in general. « It is because the tango is a dance that I have had the audacity to defend and extol it in the presence of the distinguished members of the five Academies.» And then after one of those superbly eloquent perorations for which Jean Richepin is famous — applause from even the dim-eyed old sages, delighted "murmurs" and "exclamations" from the worldlings, and a gay, enthusiastic voice from a distant corner, « Let's all of us dance the tango this very minute.»

A second Hugo

However, no tango-dancing in the severe, classical Institute of France — it was spared that lively exhibition; but the fact none the less remains that the great poet Richepin's endorsement of the tango has definitely established it in France as a dance that may be indulged in by the strictest-minded people. An Academician has extolled it and that's enough. Jean Richepin himself has admired it and such is his glory, his genius, his authority, that he holds a place in the heart of the French people second only to that of Victor Hugo. For, all his life, in poetry and prose, Richepin, like Hugo, has passionately revealed and tenderly commiserated with the woes of the poor, the innocent, the oppressed. Such indeed is the incontestability of his genius that the French Academy, the stronghold of conservatism and conventions, of militarism and Clericalism, almost unanimously accepted Richepin the independent, the large-minded and great-hearted, as a fellow Immortal. I like to recall, as an instance of French chivalry, the late François Coppée, a charming poet and a fervent Catholic, leaving his sick head to vote for Richepin. « He is an anti-Clerical, but he is a glorious poet, » frail and feeble old Coppée reiterated to the protests of his doctor. So away in his carriage — on a bitter day — wrapped on in rugs — to the Institute of France. Into it, the frail figure, supported on either side. Back, feebler than ever, to bed; a murmur of « C'est bien, je suis bien content » (« It's good, I'm very happy ») when informed of Richepin's election — and death.

The Tango is everywhere.

It was Richepin's youngest son who informed his father through the telephone that he had been created an Immortal. « Papa, papa, » shouted young Richepin hysterically « tu es elu! tu es elu! » (« you are chosen! you are chosen! »). The poet heard but could not answer; he was speechless from emotion. And he was agitated again in the day that he put on his illustrious Green Uniform for the first time and had to make his initial speech under the dome of the august Institute. So agitated that he was discovered walking up and down a dim, stony passage — nervously gesticulating, frantically reciting the opening passages of his address. « It is wretched, it will be un four noir, a black failure » — he cried despairingly. It was, as a matter of fact, one of the noblest, and most enthusiastically applauded, speeches the venerable Institute has ever heard.

So, behold the strictest French bourgeoisie involved in the tango, and the tango "admitted" into the severest corners of the Faubourg St. Germain, and tango suppers and teas on the increase in theatres and restaurants — and the boulevard journals suggesting with characteristic ribaldry that the tango should be danced at an appointed hour every day in the Chamber of Deputies, Senate, and Law Courts. Also, in every school, prison, and workhouse. Also, in the presidential palaces of the Elysée. Also, by M. Camillo Flammarion, the eminent astronomer, high up in his observatory.

Also, by Jean Richepin himself: to whom according to the same merry journalists, the music-hall managers of America have already cabled offers of £1000 a week engagement for 30 weeks."

John F. Macdonald in the Daily News.

III. The Possessed of the Tango – by Georges Goursat, 1912

Georges Goursat (aka Sem) - Les Possédées, April 1912
In Le Journal, n° 7.507 of April 15, 1913, n° 7.519 of April 28, 1913 &
n° 7.539 of May 18, 1913
https://www.elcaminito.fr/tango/21-textes/85-les-
poss%C3%A9d%C3%A9es.html

For some time, every evening, around five o'clock, one can see, in one of the main avenues of the Star, in front of a building of beautiful appearance, an unusual movement taking place, which contrasts singularly with the calm of the silent facade, with the windows turned off. Without stopping, impeccable automobiles drop off women and gentlemen of the latest chic who quickly enter the house. These furtive entries have something suspicious, clandestine, intriguing. The women especially astonish by their feverish haste. The car still slippery on the pavement, they jump out, the doors swinging, and stumbling in their tight dresses and their high heels, they rush towards the porch. As regulars, without a word, they pass in front of the box and reach the courtyard. Everything is dark there; only, at the back, the windows of a ground floor, dimly lit, let appear, through the shutters, entwined shadows, undulating to the rhythm of haunting music, which disturbs the bourgeois peace of the floors. At the first calls of this chant, the pace of these women suddenly lightens, their gait becomes rolling, balanced. Caught up in the imperious cadence as if under the impulse of an irresistible suggestion, they head for the mysterious apartment, waddling in time, quivering with impatience, until the door barely ajar, without take the time to remove their foxes, their little bag still tight, kneaded in their nervous hands, they abandon themselves to the first arms which welcome them, which watch for them.

The place is strange. It is a suite of three rooms, absolutely bare, with no other furniture than a few mismatched benches along the walls, without a rug, without curtains at the windows, without a trinket on the marble fireplaces. There is something improvised in this summary installation that denotes an unforeseen crisis, the suddenness of a passing phenomenon. In the emptiness of this sonic apartment, this music resonates strangely, tapped and scratched in a corner by a pianist and a mandolinist dazed by the obsession of this endlessly repeated rhythm. We feel that these unfortunates have been playing there for hours and hours without respite. Moved by a nervous tic, they oscillate in time on their seat, and from time to time, to wake up from their torpor, they excite and galvanize themselves by guttural cries and kicks of their heels.

In this feverish and vibrant atmosphere, men and women, whose extreme elegance contrasts with the nudity of this local vagueness, tightly coupled, modulate, meander, seem to crawl vertically against each other, like projected shadows on a shivering curtain or reflected in flowing water. Their bodies, entwined, intertwined, chest to chest and belly to belly, brushing against each other, fitting into each other by pressing, regulated and skillful twists, turn slowly, convulse almost on the spot to the accents of this sad and exalted incantation.

Unique ball! Not a laugh, not a shout, no rumor of a party. Nothing but this gloomy and agonizing music and the sliding of the feet on the parquet. These disconcerting evolutions, this tormented quasi-immobility have dance neither its anger, nor its physical joy, nor its delirium of movement. These attentive people who brush against each other, knead each other with so much stubborn and methodical application, do they practice abdominal massage? Isn't it rather a means of pleasure? Is it a sport or a vice? Are they neurotics, exhibitionists or maniacs? In front of these mysterious and lascivious contortions, one feels ill at ease, with a nervous desire to laugh, as if the hidden gesture of love were suddenly revealed in public: one even experiences this sort of frozen terror inspired by the incomprehensible mimicry of madmen. In the midst of all this disturbing unknown, we are aware of being an intruder, an undesirable, a reprobate, and we want to escape from this unclassifiable circle, which is both an opium den, the nursing home or something else…

But soon this first impression is modified, transformed. To better observe these strange dancers, their serious and absorbed air, their contained frenzy, restrained by the measured rhythm, the meticulous, calculated sobriety of their movements scrupulously respectful of the rhythm, supple, but with a precision, so to speak, liturgical; to see their ardent expression of conviction and faith, one comes to understand that they perform there a kind of sacred rite. The women are in the grip of a mystical exaltation, their gazes within, their ecstatic faces leaning forward, their eyes closed on an interior dream, serious and collected like communicants at the holy table…turning. There emanates from all their attitudes, even the most sensual, something superiorly chaste, noble, religious. I rediscovered there exactly the same indefinable confusion I felt long ago when, for the first time, I saw the whirling dervishes, in a mosque in Broussa, and it seemed to me that I was assisting, in the heart of Paris, at the office of t a sect, that I had entered into a sanctuary, one of the thousand chapels of this new cult which fascinates the city and turns heads, souls and bodies.

You guessed it, the Tango!

In Le Journal, n° 7.507 of April 15, Paris, 1913

* * *

There is no doubt that volcanoes, I was going to say the Balkans, were only created to allow Parisiennes to dance on them. Since we only talk about battles and armaments, it is singular to note that Paris is nothing more than an immense bridge of Avignon.

However, this is not the first time that we have seen Parisiennes become passionate about a dance. We have not forgotten the vogue for the cake-walk, the rage of salons and theaters, nor the [Elves?], golden, starry, beribboned puppets, who for a season were the fashionable toy, until so that Paris, sated with their stooped airs, would finish breaking them in two.

More recently, the grisly-bear, the turkey-trot and the two-steps raged, which are still in vogue. But these are only frolics of niggers on the run, innocent rage of movement, the explosions of the hectic, almost electric gaiety of this Yankee race which releases its excess of fluid and relaxes its nerves by rhythmic reflexes, sometimes waddling comically at the manner of bears, sometimes pounding the ground with hasty beats of rosin soles which squeal and vibrate in a typewriter's hurried tick-tock. But what is this unleashing of a purely physical joy, almost animal, this superficial pleasure, on edge, next to the tango, serious and passionate? It awakens in us sensations, emotions otherwise acute and complex. There is in him the mysterious force of a symbol, a magic, a spell that enchants, a charm that disturbs the soul and the senses, penetrates you to the marrow and which must have acted deeply on the nerves of these Parisiennes already intoxicated with morphine, opium or cocaine, eager for new contacts, for artificial and sterile pleasures.

You entered with me, a few days ago, into one of the secret chapels of this new rite and noted the ecstatic and religious side which makes these meetings like a kind of pagan vespers, a resurrection of the ancient mysteries of Eleusis.

Since then, this neurosis has made terrible progress. By a lightning march, it spread all over Paris, invaded salons, theaters, bars, night cabarets, large hotels and guinguettes. There are tango-teas, tango-exhibitions, tango-conferences. Half of Paris rubs shoulders with the other. The whole city is in motion: it has the tango in its skin. huge cathedrals have been dedicated to the tango where a people of fanatics, undulating, with a truly impressive unconsciousness, the swell of innumerable behinds in a trance, devote themselves, under the eyes of a thousand voyeurs, in the raw light of the lamps arched, to this alcove mimicry. In the most beautiful districts of Paris, lofty sanctuaries have been inaugurated, the porches of which are guarded by Swiss bars encased in gold, sorts of artificial skyscrapers, superimposed on four floors, all humming with guitars, crowded with convulsionaries, while the couples who have been unable to find a place in the crowded living rooms mime the Tango with their whole bodies waiting wherever they find a free corner, on the stairs, in the cloakroom, in the sinks. Moreover, everything pitches in these sumptuous cenacles of agitated people. You can hear the beads of the chandeliers tinkling, you can see the paintings oscillating on the walls, the tea in the cups vibrating. Even the bellhops at the entrance, who fetch the cars, sketching a shy waddling of their little scarlet buttocks.

But it is still in the intimacy of these modest hidden parishes, of a quite aristocratic discretion, that come, as in the catacombs, to meet the faithful, the pure, the true believers of this primitive Church. And this is where the most amazing miracles happen.

Isn't it prodigious, the spectacle of all these excessively refined people, saturated with luxury and comfort, accustomed to Ritzes and Palaces, accepting to shut themselves up regularly every afternoon in this vast room of an installation more than modest, rudimentary, and whose service is ensured only by a humble servant bewildered, of a quite evangelical simplicity? Isn't it even more surprising to see united, crammed into these three bare rooms, risking the tightest promiscuity, the most heterogeneous specimens, the most incompatible of all worlds: ferocious snobs, jealous to the point of rage of their meticulously sorted relations, aristocrats full of arrogance, imbued with all the prejudices of caste, vague vivacious, touts of casinos and chattering teeth, a princess of blood, a great man from Spain, two duchesses, actors, industrialists , officers, young girls and cranes, cosmopolitan adventurers and bourgeoises, confused in the same intoxication, the same delirium of Tango! Strange mixture, curious harlequin! All these bizarre people hug each other, embrace each other, turn and undulate, collected and serious, without shock, without disgust, with the most perfect ease and the most exquisite harmony.

These ladies and young ladies lend each other their favorite dancer, exchanging knowing half-smiles, confidences in a low voice: « Take my Pepe, princess, he's leading, it's a delight! », « You speak, Irma, if the kid is going strong! », « Oh! Fernando, what a lovely media-luna! », « My mother, if only I could catch Loulou Christi's corte! ». And the young girl, under the eyes of the tender mother, abandons herself to the arms of Loulou's regular dancer; she finds herself, in contact with the rough cheviotte of the suit, impregnated with the evocative and forbidden perfume, on the supple body of the Argentinian still vibrating from the previous tango, a remnant of the initiating ardor of the pretty artist who has just swoon over it.

And besides, do not doubt it, these young people, after having mixed their breath, their perspiration, their juice, tangled their knees, braided their legs, melted their flesh bristling with desire, after having been mixed, amalgamated, tossed for hours by the gentle mechanism of this musical churning, will resume, on leaving, with their cloakroom, their prejudices, their disdain and their distances, and – having shaken off this bewitchment in the salubrious air outside – will not know each other more.

Where does this prestigious Tango come from? Who is the propagating apostle of this strange rite? Who inoculated us with the microbe of this neurosis? I tried to clarify this little point of Parisian history, to understand the origin of this epidemic and to follow its evolution.

And first, let's clarify. There is tango and tango.

The Spanish tango, with boleros and castanets, as old-fashioned as Otero and Tertojada, is no more than an old, worn tambourine, a dusty memory of the party favors of yesteryear.

Only exists the Argentine Tango, the idol of the day.

Everyone knows that the gauchos, half-shepherds, half-picadors, herders of oxen and tamers of horses, are the peasants of Argentina, which has not always been the country of model "estancias", so brilliantly described by Jules Huret. Barely half a century ago, the pampas stretched out, a vast desert of grassland, where these fierce peasants dressed in leather, shod in terribly spurred boots, led a nomadic and savage life.

Like the shepherds of all times and all countries, from Virgil's Tityre to the Berbers of our day, who walk their sheep on the high plateaus of the Atlas, to the little brown shepherd in his red beret in the green softness of the evenings on the Dordogne, these gauchos liked, at the end of the day, to exhale in sad and simple songs the vague daydreams of their elementary souls, so close to nature, undergoing, like the oxen which moo at the agony of the sun, the melancholy of twilight.

It was on the Spanish guitar that they found the accents of a serious and passionate melody, characterized by a very special rhythm which recalls a little the habanera and also the sad and wild songs of the aboriginal Indians. The peasants of the country call this rhythm the milonga.

Well, the tango is only a derivation, a development of this theme, and it is in the milonga that we must recognize the very rustic origin of this dance which upsets elegant Paris. Here we are far from the learned contortions of the pretty ladies and their beautiful Argentinians with lacquered hair.

Let's abbreviate.

The tango, from the depths of the countryside, reached Buenos-Ayres, with the convoys of oxen escorted to the capital by these bards of the Pampas. They played it and danced it in the taverns near the slaughterhouses, and we will see in a final article this lullaby melody of the dreams of solitaries, this pastoral dance deteriorates in contact with the low population of the hovels, and degenerate, degraded by the contortions obscene, to the point of becoming a kind of Argentinian swaying.

In Le Journal, n° 7.519 of April 28, Paris, 1913

* * *

At the risk of being excommunicated, and braving anathemas, I dare to profane an idol and secularize the divine tango. But before daring this iconoclastic gesture, I hesitate, seized with scruples. Why turn off the sanctuary lamp and not leave this dance, which does no harm to anyone, quite the contrary, its poetic pastoral legend, its wild scent of the pampas? Why be the sinister obstacle to pitching in circles? Alas! it is my duty as a historian to ruthlessly tell the impure truth, which my previous article gave you a glimpse of, and I am going to ask forgiveness in advance for the nice convictions that I am going to offend, the charming illusions that I am going to wither. Buenos-Ayres, as everyone knows, is a superb city almost entirely new, of which the Argentinians are justly proud. But its incredible prosperity is relatively recent, and there still remains, the last vestige of the primitive city, a filthy suburb, picturesquely acrid and violent, which bears the significant name of Barrio de las ranas (suburb of the frogs). This district, where low prostitution is relegated and where the slums and brothels of the last category are grouped, recalls from afar the old Riddeck of Antwerp or the Red Hat of Toulon. But what gives this place a unique aspect is the unexpected architecture of the buildings that rise there. You have to imagine that these bastringues are only built with oil drums and tin cans. All this clattering tinsmithing, cut into rosettes, slashed into festoons, spirals and lambrequins, manages to create sorts of baroque palaces, mad alhambras, absurd Eldorados, whose facades streaked with multicolored labels: Standard oil, Corned beef, Chicago, Azucar de Tucuman, shimmer fiercely in the sun with all the fires of their tinning shining with oil, fat and molasses. Around these sticky Eden rise real mounds of filth, heaps of carcasses, rotten fish, debris of all kinds, teeming with rats and vermin, dumped there every day in cartloads, and which the municipality, by hygienic measure, burn on low heat. From these foul hearths rise whirlwinds of pungent smoke, the stench of which is aggravated by the grating of the eateries in the open air. The heaping up in this same rotting pit of all the social dross thrown up by this enormous fermenting city, alongside the heap of rubbish from its roads, composes a picture of truly Dantesque horror, and this setting, made up of smoking hills of The rubbish, of putrid volcanoes, is well suited to this tinsel Suburre which appears, all resounding with the rabid din of orchestrions and mechanical organs, like a hideous fair of the most abject lust.

The population that haunts these dens is largely made up of the waste of Italian immigration, a whole low Latinity, mixed with Indians, scum from the ports of the Mediterranean. These Argentinian Apaches, who are reminiscent, but very high in tone, of the ruffians of Naples and the nervis of Marseilles, bear, in the slang of Buenos-Ayres, the name of "compadritos". Very dark, with a complexion of oil soup, their faces are shaved with blood, except for a thin cosmetic mustache. Wearing a felt hat pulled down over their dark eyes, they wear very pomaded hair, quite long and cut neat on the carefully shaved neck. This bare neck makes them even more sinister by giving them the vague air of having undergone the executioner's toilet. Dressed in short jacket and wide trousers that fall over very high-heeled boots, their shirts sparkling with fake sparkles, they realize the type of rastaquouère thug. But what is particularly interesting in relation to the tango that concerns us, is the character of their approach and their attitudes. Eyes on the lookout, spying on the police or supervising the work of their females, they glide along the hovels with a sly, elastic suppleness, of felines in a cage, their backs brushing against the walls to guard against some treacherous attack, advancing, oblique and sly, with an oblique step, the belly in offering, the bending legs, gathered up on themselves, as if ready to pounce. They are the true creators of the Argentine tango, which is only the development of their pace disciplined by a rhythm and transformed into a dance. It is this basely lascivious swaying that they continue in the tango in which they indulge with their "putas" [hookers], at the back of the dens, to charm the tricks of the trade or entice the clientele. We find, in fact, in the variations of the corte all the characteristics of this gait, of this "meneo" [swaying], as the Spaniards say, the same oblique steps with joined knees, the same lustful contortions, aggravated by cynically precise jerks, all the simian obscenity of Indian dances. The Tango is only the belly dance for two, the so to speak professional dance of the lupanars of Uruguay and Argentina. Well, dear madam, don't mind, these are the only salons in Buenos-Ayres where your divine Tango triumphs; and you would recoil in horror in the face of these repugnant realities, in front of these oily compadritos which, to the accents of the sad milonga, convulse ignobly, a red carnation stuck behind the ear, dropping from their rogue mouth, where a cigarette butt smolders, jets of brown saliva squirting over the shoulder of their swooning "niñas" [girls], glued to them! As a result of what misunderstanding this shameless dance, benefiting from the vogue, the prestige of everything that comes to us from Latin America, was it adopted by Paris without control? By what aberration is the tango, whose name alone makes a second-class demi-mondaine blush in Buenos-Ayres, be welcomed here with open arms by the best society and danced in the most purist salons? Happy puzzle! It is true that between Argentina and France there is an abyss, the ocean, and that this exotic fruit, a little too spicy for our climates, had time, during its twenty-five days of pitching, to disgorge its venom and evaporate its musk in the purifying breath of the sweet trade wind. But all the same it is a miracle to see how French women, with their exquisite sense of proportion, have been able to transform and perfect it; and I am delighted, after this debauchery of frightful descriptions, to recognize that in Paris certain women of the world and even of the demi dance the Tango, a Tango a little watered down, a little parigoté, with a decent and light grace, an air of hardly touching it, a little pinch-to-spray kind of the best tone, where the tact and the taste of these parties are manifested, which knew how to make this wild swaying an elegant flirtation of slender and discreet legs. They avenge us, these true Parisiennes, of all the other possessed women who, denying the Faubourg Saint-Germain for that of the Grenouilles, pitch shamelessly with the cadence of a springer. As for the French, very few manage to equal the mastery of the Argentinians and the Spaniards. Their style is too ornate, too loaded with frills, not focused enough. Too much zeal, gentlemen owners! Your anxious buttocks, watching the measure, wrinkled like peach pits from all the moires of attention and stubborn worry. It is a joy! Ah! really! too much seriousness, too much faith, too much worship! Let us burst out laughing thinking that the tangos which, in Buenos-Ayres, bear the names of owners as titles: La Laura, La Queca, or alcove remarks of this juice: "Morde me la camisa!" (Bite me the shirt), are baptized, in Paris, with sweet and kind little names, like Loulou or Primerose. And the terrible gaucho Simarro [Bernabé Simara], with his sharp profile like a tomahawk beak, oh! Paris, what have you done? A kind of Fouquières from the pampa who can be seen every night on the pink carpet of fashionable restaurants, flanked by gypsies in frogs, fluttering in frantic entrechats his wide embroidered calico trousers in the face of delighted soup maids ready to prostrate before the starry rowels of his enormous silver spurs as before the rays of a monstrance.

The tango of Paris, you see, is the skin of a stinking animal arriving from the depths of Siberia, soiled and infected with miasma, being transformed, in the magic hands of the furriers, until it becomes the precious sable, warm caress and perfumed with the fragile shoulders of Parisiennes; it is the black and juicy Havana, metamorphosed into a thin blond and golden cigarette; the Tango de Paris is the denicotinized Argentine Tango. And when it crosses the ocean again, you will no longer recognize it, beautiful ladies from Buenos-Ayres, your tango de las ranas. It will come back to you adorned with all the graces of Paris, perfumed, wavy, adorably crumpled, article of the rue de la Paix."

In Le Journal, n° 7.539 of May 18, Paris, 1913

* * *

Georges Goursat*

*Georges Goursat (1863–1934), known as Sem, was a French caricaturist famous during the Belle Epoque. In 1900, he self-published a new album, Le Turf, with caricatures of many prominent Parisian socialites (Marquess Boni de Castellane, Prince Trubetskoy, Count Clermont-Tonnerre, Baron Alphonse and Gustave de Rothschild, Polaire). The success of this album made him famous overnight. Ten others followed until 1913.

IV. The Tango in Paris – by Carlos Pereyra, 1913

El Tango en París
Por Carlos Bareiro Pereyra
La revista Fray Mocho, no.48, 28 Marzo 1913
https://digital.iai.spk-berlin.de/viewer/image/863753094/51/
https://digital.iai.spk-berlin.de/viewer/image/863753094/52/

When people comment in Buenos Aires about the celebrity that tango con corte has reached in Paris - the most popular of our Creole dances — no one even suspects the exact measure of its proportions.

In reality, this vogue has become a true fervor, a "chronic disease", as a popular fashion magazine said, in a cheerful tone a few days ago.

Among all and above all modern dances, the tango stands out from Paris with the attributes of undisputed supremacy. Neither the "Pas de l'Ours", nor the "One Step" of the Yankees, nor the same "Double Boston", which add up to an incalculable number of followers, have managed to rival for a moment the dance of the compadres from Buenos Aires.

The Argentine tango grants here a patent of supreme distinction. A fashionable man, a "chic" gentleman, would consider himself very tarnished if he were forced to confess that he is unfamiliar with the art of embroidering arabesques on the glossy "parquet" of dance halls, leading a gentile couple, who by the way bearing and by the intense fire that burst from her pupils through the silks of her half-closed eyelashes, she constantly reminds us of the graceful brunettes of our payments.

His difficulties and how expensive his learning is, have prevented tango from that vulgarization that always tends to aristocratic prestige of all fashions.

Thanks to such conditions, their domains are perhaps relatively small, but, on the other hand, they are among the most select. In effect, it will be a vain attempt to go looking for tangoists at the "Tabarin", at the "Moulin Rouge", at the "Moulin de la Galette" or in other similar places, where the modest prices allow the infiltration of elements subaltern and even crooks, and where the concurrence, consequently, offers a heterogeneous character.

At the very least, you have to go up to "Magic City", the place consecrated to the "rendez vous" of the elegant world, whose beautiful building stands on the Pont du Alma, on the banks of the Seine and the Eiffel Tower whose salon brings together the tango "amateurs" at every Monday and Thursday.

They are in the "cafés de nuit" and in the "houses of soupers", where the cheapest consummation always mounts a Luis [a Brazilian Luis Duque], who dances the Argentine tango every night, from 12 to 4 am. Its owners, in order to satisfy the demands of the clientele, have had to hire "danseurs" and "danseuses" for salons, tango, who, naturally, as they are counted, earn fabulous wages, collect blonde tips, only eat like Lucullus ate and better perhaps, and they are the true spoiled children of those places where they are disputed, if they are men, by women; if women, men.

The "Aboye", "Le Rat Morte", the "Pigalle-Soupers", the "Féria", the "Capitole" ... Here are a few famous restaurants in the annals of Montmartre, true temples of gold and pleasures, in those for which access is conditional ("l'habillement negligée on refuse rigourosement") and very expensive, where the "elite" Parisians have circumscribed tango to defend it from the contagion of excessive popularity!

A very eloquent demonstration, perhaps, of this incredible celebrity, is the fact that a Brazilian machicha teacher, Mr. Luis Duque, has just opened on rue Fontaine, on the upper floors of the Deux-Masques theater, an artistic Cabaret that has been baptized in the name of "El Tango", a name that performs the trade of a true imam, because thanks to him, in a few days, the fame of the new establishment has been made.

On the other hand, M. Camille de Rhynal, a dance teacher awarded by the International Academy and one of the best tangoists in Paris, has contracted the great hall of the "Magic City" for three years for the matinees that I have mentioned before.

He, personally, has confessed to me that the business yields results that he did not even dare to think about the first days.

Another detail that can help measure the celebrity of tango in Paris is the number of times competitions are held between amateurs and teachers. Indeed, it is not yet four months since the one organized by the "Excelsior" newspaper was held and another 25 of the current one has already been carried out at the Folie Magic theater, organized by the aforementioned M. Camille de Rhynal.

A large and select audience attended the festival. The prize in the teachers' contest went to Bernabé Simara, the "black", as his friends call him in Buenos Aires, or the "king of tango", as he is called here, along with his partner, a beautiful and already famous dancer. Cuban, Miss Ideal Gloria.

The first prize for "amateurs" also went to an Argentine, Mr. Pirovano.

Bernabé Simara a unique type for tango. Already in Buenos Aires, since 1909, he did not recognize a rival who could compete, with him in the art of sit-downs and half-moons, as evidenced by the first prizes of the Casino, the Royal and the Politeama, which he won in the annual carnival contests.

He came to Paris with Mlle. Papillon, an artist who learned to dance with him and hired them to work together.

Today Simara's fame equals that of the most renowned artists. He earns 1,200 francs a month as a professor at the Academie Rhynal, the best known in Paris, where he works two hours a day; 30 or 40 francs at the Abeye Restaurant for each soirée, not counting the tips that sometimes add up to more than the pay, and then, dinners, champagne and the sea...

He will soon, accompanied by the "charmante" Ideal Gloria, he will dance for a synchronized "film", hired by a well-known film company.

See if the profession is enviable or not.

And although in truth the gallantry of race does not have a greater reason to boast for this, it is always satisfying to verify that in Paris they know that Argentines exist, even if it is because of the shore tango.

Carlos BAREIRO PEREYRA

Paris, February 1913.

V. The Tango in Buenos Aires – by Enrique Carrillo, 1914

THE TANGO
chapter of the book "The Charm of Buenos Aires"
Enrique Carrillo, 1914
https://archive.org/details/elencantodebueno00gmez/page/181/mode
/1up?ref=ol&view=theater&q=Tango

It is a remote, sordid and almost deserted neighborhood. On the ground, full of water, the strange lights of the street lighting are reflected with spectral lividities. Along the sidewalk, true "path", as they say here, we marched, jumping over the puddles, the three guests of the man who best knows the suburbs of Buenos Aires. In front, making noble speeches on popular music, goes Blasco Ibáñez**. Behind him, silent and nervous, walks Emilio Thuillier. I try not to abandon our gentle cicerone.

« Of course, it won't be like what you saw in Paris, » he exclaims. « For that you must go to the downtown cabarets, where the girls from France ... »

But they are not girls from France, no, nor are they refined and stylized graces that we want to see, but natural flowers from the Buenos Aires mud and riverbank undulations.

« You'll see, » he murmurs.
Then, excusing himself:
— Only that you are going to notice the difference... Here they dance without art... Tango, as the Europeans have transformed it, is a much more elegant dance than that of our compadritos. What I want to show you now is a very ordinary thing... You see the neighborhood ...
More than ordinary is, in effect, the den into which we have just entered ... It is a vast room without any decoration, without even paper on the walls and barely lit by a few gas burners. In the background, in a kind of wooden cage, six musicians prepare their instruments. Crowded around a few dirty tables, a hundred patrons drink, chat, laugh. At first it is difficult to notice what people look like. The men, thin and young in general, with their bowler hats and long hair trailing behind, seem to respond to what is called the "compadrito" type. Women form a more heterogeneous humanity. There are those who turn out to be true children, with their large candid eyes wide open in their rosy faces, and there are those who have the faces of grandmothers: in such a way the age is marked in the wrinkles of their cheeks. But the most disturbing — and the most interesting too — are neither these nor those, but the thin, pale, haggard and serpentine girls, who, with a uniform smile, look at everyone who enters in a spectral and provocative way.

« Curious, » murmurs Thuillier — « Great! » exclaims Blasco Ibáñez**.

Our guide takes me to the musicians' cage to offer me a chair and to order a tango.

« These creatures, » he tells me, « are, morally and materially, the lowest thing in Buenos Aires. To discover them, it is necessary to come here, to the banks of the river. Look at their suits, and you'll notice how little the poor wretches know about luxury and fashion. »

The showy rags of the sinners are, indeed, as varied as their types. There are fat women who proudly flaunt Claudine costumes, exposing their round calves with an air that wants to be childish and is nothing but infamous. There are young women, very painted and very flirtatious, who perform the sad miracle of looking elegant with rags from ten years ago. There are some, naive and gentle, who join a dance bodice to a "tailleur" skirt. And there are those who, renouncing all struggle, proclaim, with their pitiful abandon, the misery of supreme defeats.
My cicerone begins to point out some who were once gallant stars.

« Here » he tells me « Life is faster than in Europe... Beauty lasts less... Fortune, too... »

The preludes of the orchestra force him to be silent. From the humble violin's springs, with weighted and subtle languor, the delicious rhythm of tango. It is the same that I have heard all over the world, at all hours; It is the classic tango, the best known by the people, the one that even the street organs of Guatemala already know how to play. But, far from complaining about not hearing something new, I am glad that it is with such notes, which are the same ones that serve the beautiful Parisians at their parties, with which we are going, at last, to see the Buenos Aires dance in its manifestation more original and more suburban.
Here comes, slow and measured, a couple... Then another, which seems to follow the first... Then others, not many: ten or twelve... And they pass before my observatory without haste, without violence, almost without enthusiasm, counting the steps, preparing for the cuts, taking care not to make mistakes... And little by little the atmosphere warms up, not with the fiery life of the clubs of Madrid's Bombilla, where couples embrace in tight embraces, but with the artificial and somewhat theatrical fever of Parisian "teas". Because, despite what almost everyone says, the dance is the same here, in its cradle of mud, as it is in the golden palaces to which it has been transplanted by European fashion.

Seeing the couples go by and review, I wonder what the reasons could be why this dance has provoked, not only the anathemas of the bishops, but also the questioning of Buenos Aires society.

« Oh!... Tango! » - exclaim the ladies of Buenos Aires, as if it were something monstrous.

And when someone says that in an Argentine embassy there has been a night out, His Excellency the Ambassador, Rodriguez Larreta, sends a cable to the Government and the press of his country protesting against such slander that stains the reputation of our ladies, has written one of the most distinguished spirits of the country.

That?... On the contrary. That, in the bouge where before we only saw misery and vice, tension and sleaze, has created, with the magic of its slow and stately rhythm, which seems to lengthen the silhouettes and refine the waistlines, an atmosphere of gallant, worldly party and measured. I no longer recognize, in effect, in these couples either the compadritos with the fungus over their ears or the sad sinners in crazy rags. Without linking up, almost without touching, looking more at their steps than at their faces, the one and the other smile with a serious smile, the same on all lips, and undulate in complicated steps, as if they were celebrating a rite of ceremonious harmonies. Where is the sin, where is the perversity, where is the lewdness in this dance? What's more: where is the voluptuous abandon of the waltzes?...

The Tango...

There is, without a doubt, a terrible and magnificent tango that is not only the pantomime of love, like many other dances, but also the palpitating image of spasm. It is the Spanish tango, made of shocks, tremors, tensions and voluptuous agonies. A few nights ago, in the heart of Buenos Aires, in one of the most elegant theaters, before a very distinguished audience, I saw a girl from Seville who was dancing flamenco tangos. It was a beautiful spectacle, surely, before which, without realizing it, the audience was intoxicated with voluptuousness. "Long live your mother!" — shouted the simple gallants of the galleries. And hearing the exclamation so Spanish, I thought that that girl, almost anonymous, could very well be a daughter of La Puga, fine and naked, to whom Barrés consecrated one of his Cadiz madrigals. Oh yeah! All the sacred instinct of pure and wild love throbbed in her petite person, and her ring-shaped beauty, trembling at the impulse of an indomitable instinct, put, like a purple host, on the lips of her one-night admirers, the sublime sensation of what that never changes: of desire, of pleasure, of vertigo... But apart from the name, what does Andalusian tango, barbaric, sublime and pathetic, have in common with its brother, Argentine tango, fine, feline and courteous?...

The dance that I see tonight in this "bouge" of Buenos Aires, and which is the same one I have seen before in Parisian salons, far from embodying the religious triumph of the healthy and strong popular Venus, personifies study, self-control, wise application and refined artifice. There is not a note in it, not a rhythm, not a step, not a gesture, not an attitude, that are natural, that are frank, that have been born from the earth covered with loving sweat, like a wildflower. Even the mere indication that, according to the technical phrase, it is a dance to "setback", indicates its affected and learned character. But this is not all. Every detail, every movement, every figure, every undulation, every swing, is of a very affected wisdom.

Is it true that this dance is the one danced by ranchers in the pampas and by sailors in the brothels of the farthest ports of Buenos Aires? People believe it because the newspapers say so. But I cannot, logically, accept it. Country people and provincial plebs have no time to learn complicated dances. More than suburban, for the rest, tango seems to come out of some hotel in Rambouillet of choreographic art: in such a way as a whole it is a paragon of soft preciousness and elegant complications. In our century, positive and brief, even something anachronistic results with its thirty-two different figures or steps. Seeing it well, without prejudice, one says to oneself:

— This dance is a brother of those languid pavanes and those ceremonious minuets of the eighteenth century. It is a court dance... An anecdote shows the difficulties of tango, as well as its purity.

When Richepin began to write his theatrical play "Tango", the two actresses who were to play the leading roles, Mademoiselle Lavalliére and Mademoiselle Spinelly, set about learning the new dance. The night of the premiere, however, some knowledgeable spectators noticed that what the two pretty Parisians were dancing was not tango. Questioned by Le Matin, Mademoiselle Lavalliere replied:

« It's what we dance, it's a kind of matchicha... tango is too difficult to learn in a few weeks... and, besides, it's not voluptuous enough... »

Certain. The Argentine tango, as it is practiced in Paris, is a slow, elegant, distinguished, aristocratic, chaste and complicated dance. The couples measure the steps with extraordinary care. At the slightest mistake, all is lost. Each gesture corresponds to a severe and invariable rule. And there is not one of her movements, well, one, that the purest lady cannot execute. But the strange thing, the inexplicable thing, is that the tango that I see tonight in this low and vile "bouge" of Buenos Aires does not differ from the Parisian tango in any essential detail. Luna-Park dancers are definitely more beautiful, more luxurious, more graceful and graceful than the ones here. The dance is the same.

Could such a phenomenon consist in the fact that the influence of Parisian refinement has already reached such a miserable and distant suburb?...

I ignore it.

Our guide, however, remains convinced that he has just made us see a very vulgar show, and excuses himself by telling us again.

« This is not Paris... »

And when I assure him that I see no difference between the denigrated tango of La Boca and the adored tango of Montmartre or the Champs Elysée, he exclaims:

« It seems like a lie! »

He doesn't see that this is a most rude, most plebeian dance... (1). — what seems incredible — he replied — is that it is a popular dance, when it seems made for court ceremonies...

(1) At the last minute I find, in an unfair article by Leopoldo Lugones, a jasta phrase. Here it is, dated Paris and written in French:

« Seulement le tango, j'y insiste, se danse ici comme labas. » (« Only the tango, I insist, is danced here as there. »)

It is true ... And here (Buenos Aires) and there (Paris) the tango is delightful, my dear beloved and great poet.

Enrique Carrillo*

*Enrique Carrillo (February 27, 1873, in Guatemala City – November 29, 1927, in Paris) was a Guatemalan literary critic, writer, journalist and diplomat, and the second husband of the Salvadoran French writer and artist Consuelo Suncin de Sandoval-Cardenas, later Consuelo Suncin, Comtesse de Saint Exupery, who in turn was his third wife; he had been previously married to intellectual Aurora Caceres and Spanish actress Raquel Meller.

** Vicente Blasco Ibáñez (January 29, 1867 – January 28, 1928) was a journalist, politician and bestselling Spanish novelist in various genres whose most widespread and lasting fame in the English-speaking world is from Hollywood films that were adapted from his works as "Blood and Sand" and "The Four Horsemen of Apocalypse" who made Rudolph Valentino famous as a tango dancer!

Figure 4: "Le Tango" Mr & Mrs Jean Richepin and Dancers, 1913

2 THE TANGO ORIGIN

The opera "Carmen" by the French composer Georges Bizet, which it was premiered in March 1875, it contains some of the most underrated secrets of the origins of the Tango. The Carmen's aria of Habanera was based in the older Cuban Tango "El Arreglito", and later the Habanera itself served as the base for the most famous Argentine Tango, the "El Choclo". As well, Carmen represented the Spanish Tango culture that immigrated to Argentina.

A deep review of those cultures is a necessary condition to understand how the Tango was born:

I. The African roots

II. The Caribbean connection

III. The South American influence

IV. The European infusion

V. The melting pot of Buenos Aires

I. The African roots

One of the main creative foundations of tango dance derives from African traditional and ceremonial dances. The African dance aesthetic is evident through much of early tango dance expression and forms the foundation for the aesthetic (technical) and kinetic (physical) expression of delivery. Music is the fundamental creative seed that drives the dance and interpretation of movement. Not forgetting that the purpose behind the African tradition is a collective expression through which the dance and the music are a natural extension and creative reflection of everyday life, real life.

Throughout Africa, all tribes have their own individual dances and traditions, which are passed down to each generation. Dance and music are not separated from everyday life; they are party to all sacred and social functions, and the creative underpinning of the community. African dance is complete in its delivery. It is performed by the community to celebrate birth, weddings, death and the marking of rites of passage. Competitive dance (challenges/battles) is also part of the structure, the re-telling of ancestral history or poetry (griots) and finding a closer connection to God (spiritual). There is a great emphasis on the collective and the community, allowing for audience and performers to participate and contribute to the whole experience (inclusive). African dance is all-inclusive and is recognized and reflected as both a sacred and secular form of cultural and creative expression.

African dance cannot be viewed as one simple form of dance expression. There are many differences between the tribal groups and regional dances of Africa, which dictate the dances physical aesthetic and delivery.

Each region of African dance has a specific emphasis on the physical expression and movement. For example, in Ghana, the upper body is a predominant feature within the physical movement. In regions such as Nigeria, the emphasis is accentuated through hips and pelvis. The African tribe of the Maasai are known for their athletic legs, jumps and elevation, and then there is the intricate footwork and hand clapping that is akin to the Akan traditions of Ghana.

African dance has three distinct attributes:

a) Polyrhythmic: the connectivity between the physical expression and interpretation of dance movement to the intricate, crossed rhythms and accents within the music.

b) Polycentrism: denotes the dexterity to subdivide the body movements, using differing parts of the body at the same time. This quality is aligned to the differing layers and sounds in the music and musical instrumentation.

c) Improvisation - the immediate expression of dance and movement without preparation, creating a spontaneous physical and emotional connection and individual creative expression to the music.

These are recognizable attributes in the physical expression of African dance. However, it is through the relationship to the music that the dance takes on another direction of energy, communication and connectivity. The core essence of African creative culture and tradition is through dance and music, which are innately and instinctively connected and part of everyday life.

African dance is very versatile in conception and execution. There are no restrictions to the body and physical movement, therefore, African dance can be presented and performed in varying ways: from slow and controlled in movement (lyrical), to the most spontaneous and dynamic of movement, evolving through intuitive performance (improvisation). The dance can also be performed to show power and strength (warrior/tribal dances), to offering a peaceful transition in death and honoring the Gods (ceremonial and ring dances). This is bound together through acknowledging cultural traditions that strengthens the bond within the community (storytelling/singing/call and response).

II. The Caribbean connection

The Caribbean geographically is a group of islands in the Caribbean Sea that spans over the south-east of the Gulf of Mexico, east of Central America and north of South America. It includes the islands of Cuba, Hispaniola, Haiti, Jamaica, Grenada, Carriacou, Dominican Republic, Trinidad and Tobago and many others.

Caribbean dance evolved from complex influences, due to European colonization of the islands by the British, French, Spanish, Portuguese and Dutch. It followed that the indigenous folk dances would certainly be influenced by European dance styles and music. The Africans, brought to work on the plantations, continued to hold on to their creative customs and drumming traditions, but also adopted the dances of the indigenous population on the Islands. The indigenous people of some of the Islands, called Arawaks or the Taino people, originated from mainland South America, but found homelands on the islands of the Caribbean. The traditional dances that are still observed on the islands include the kumina and tambu from Jamaica, the bele from Martinique and, from Haiti, the voodoo dances.

Through the dances and music of the Caribbean, the direct lineage to the traditions and connections of African dance and music continued to live. Plantation dances, such as the bamboula, juba, voodoo, calinda and the chica, were slave dances performed on the plantations by both men and women. European dances taken to the Islands include the quadrilles, square dances, cotillions, alongside the more courtly or classical dances of the time such as the gavotte, minuet and sarabande. The Caribbean islands that danced the quadrille continued to evidence the traditional dances and customs directly linked to Africa, by developing their own characteristic adaptations. The structure gave rise to many versions of the Caribbean quadrille.

III. The South American Influence

It is sometimes forgotten that African slaves were transported to both North and South America. It was the Portuguese who began the forced movement of African slaves to Brazil and other parts of South America throughout the sixteenth century. The African traditions and cultural expressions, musical rhythms and physical aesthetics resonate throughout Latin American dance forms. The dances recognizable from this region of the world include the rumba, a style of dance that originates from the musical pulse of the African drum. It is a fast-moving, hip-swinging and competitive dance, always accompanied by fast-paced drum music, alongside more traditional Latin instruments, such as maracas, the clave and shakers. Over time this evolved into the chica dance. The chica dance has a direct lineage to the Africa tribal dances of the Congo. It was a dance performed for processions (marching) and religious ceremonies. A descendent of the chica dance is the dance of the fandango. The mamba (also called 'mambo' meaning 'conversation with the gods') originated in Cuba from the Haitians of African descendants. The mamba is a spiritual and religious dance and music ceremony and tradition that evokes the spirit 'voodoo' of the high priestess mamba.

It is important to recognize that much of African dance had a specific meaning. Consequently, the power of this type of dance enabled the survival of the African and Caribbean traditions, both in dance and music. This can be clearly recognized today in most Afro-Latin dance styles, including the samba, merengue and calypso. The social dance element continues to keep the Latin connection very much part of the tango journey, both for the non-professional and professional dancer.

IV. The European Infusion

European dance is traditionally viewed as a secular and status art form. The development and practice of the dances descend from two distinctive styles of dance and expression: court/classical dances (upper class) and folk dances (lower class).

Classical dance (ballet) first appeared in the Italian courts of the sixteenth century and then became popular in France during the reign of Louis XIV. Much of the dance technique formed in the seventeenth century set in place the origins of classical dance. Among the formal courtly dances from Baroque and Renaissance dance of the seventeenth century were the minuet, gavotte, waltz, quadrille or contredanse and cotillion.

Folk dances of European descent that originate from the indigenous people are recognized as informal dances, such as the clog dances, Irish jig, morris dance, pole dancing, Scottish lilts, polka, gypsy and flamenco dance. These dances were often perceived as non-technical dances of the working-class community.

An interesting observation is that the European court dances presented a visual non-transferable expression, whilst folk dance presented a physical and creative expression of the community - no different in purpose to that of the traditional African dances.

V. The melting pot of Buenos Aires

The roots of tango dance can easily be identified by the three-dance expression: African dance, South American dance and European dance. Each offers something unique, yet wholly individual, to the tango dance story. It is from this unique social interaction and cross fertilization that the tango vernacular has been afforded a foundation from which to grow, over time developing into one of the most popular and influential dance forms of the past two hundred plus years.

In 1925, the Argentine (Russian immigrant) Count Juan Eugenio de Chikoff, the inventor of the tango step "1— 2, 3, 4 close and cross", had been very requested by the media and had collaborated in several magazine articles and radio interviews.

Juan Eugenio de Chikoff (1896-1988) never forgot the education he received in Czarist Russia and defended his noble origins.

Juan Eugenio de Chikoff (Bessarabia, August 29, 1896 - Buenos Aires, December 28, 1988) was a Russian exiled, dance teacher, good manners, among other disciplines, and introduced the "tango de salón" in the Argentine high society.

It was born in a predominantly Rumanian region with an ethnic mosaic at that time controlled by the Russian Empire and currently divided between Moldavia and Ukraine called Bessarabia (although he claimed to be from Moscow) in 1896, son of Miguel de Chikoff and Tatiana Youssoupoff.

He fought in the First World War in France for 19 years, in 1915, as an infantry officer. He was surprised by the Bolshevik Revolution of 1917 because he did not return to Russia.

Convinced by a friend, he travels to Argentina to wait for the Bolsheviks' fall. In this country he began to introduce himself into the Buenos Aires aristocracy and became famous for his social culture, good modalities and European courtesy.

On March 23, 1917, he marries Adélaïde Baechtel in Buenos Aires (Bischoffsheim in Alsace, February 16, 1893-Mutzig in Alsace, January 4, 1967). He was father of two children: Jorge and Eugenia de Chikoff, and the family returned to Europe. After separating from his wife, he returned definitively to Argentina.

In 1920, Chikoff had already achieved a certain relevance in society, and gave skating classes on ice, dance and gymnasium at the Golf Club of Mar del Plata, among other places. He also began to impart lessons in urbanity and in how to behave in a modern society; themes to which he would dedicate a large part of his life.

He was also who started to give tango lessons, quitting a little the close contact and passion proper of the suburbs and brothels, creating the tango de salón and introducing it in the high classes. He created the step "one, two, three, four, close and cross". This work carried out by Chikoff was valid since he had his own radio audition to teach how to dance, and a tango took his nickname "Chikoff" written by the Catalan Manuel Jovés.

According to a periodical article published in the daily newspaper La Nación, the count of Chikoff spoke nine languages, he was an aviator, journalist, sportsman, horse-rider and dancer.

« He taught everything: ice skating, roller skating, horse riding, aviation, tango… » — said his daughter Eugenia de Chikoff — « He invented the tango step '1— 2, 3, 4 close and cross' — like it or not —, but they didn't recognize it because, they didn't like it that a Russian had pulled out of the tango from the suburbs and polished it so that they could dance it in Barrio Norte of the Argentina high society. »

In 1926, an interview was transcribed on the radio by Count Juan Eugenio de Chikoff carried out in 1925, and published in the magazine "El Hogar", on December 10, 1926:

"TESTIMONIES TO THE HISTORY OF TANGO
The truth is that something must exist within the tango. All new dances are held. triumph. And goodbye! The wind takes them away…

Only the tango keeps falling, making drawings on the carpet like the butterflies of the spring that, according to Fabre, live in many winters…

The tango, therefore, as an element of human life, provides the wise with philosophical arguments. The first to give the voice of alarm had been the conductor of the dance, the Argentine Count Juan Eugenio de Chikoff, which, a year ago, exposed by radiotelephony his impressions of the tango.

« El tango, » he says, more or less, « is the father, mother and son of all modern dances. »

There are so many harmonies, so many figures and so much heart, that the fox-trot, the blues and the charleston, are nothing more than loans from the tango. Through all the modern dances, a teacher of aesthetics could easily see, as with Roentgen rays, that the Argentine tango is the skeleton of these dances. That is to say: always the tango, dressed in the Yankee style, the English style, on the rue de la Paix. Always the same tango with different surnames.

Many will ask:

— But, in fact, is tango Argentine?

It seems that the music came with the candombés on the slave ships that arrived from the Congo.

But tango, as a dance, was improvised in America — in the old colonial Buenos Aires —, whose blacks, to the beat of the drum, jumped and made dengues, sprains and gestures, without pretending to dance, but… dancing.

When Count Juan E. de Chikoff was consulted, he told us:

— He listened to a version that seems to me to be the most accurate. He attributes the beginnings of the tango to the dances of colonial service during the viceroyalty. I have heard a version that seems to me the most accurate. He attributes the beginnings of the tango to the dances of the colonial servitude during the viceroyalty. Coloured people congregated in boisterous festivals. They drank and sang without moderation. When the joy of the party reached its paroxysm, the attendees, inspired by alcohol, improvised to the rhythm of the African drum, a lewd and messy dance, in which the feet of the dancers tried to follow the syncopated rhythm of the black music.

— And the name of tango?

— It seems that he is not African. He was born in Buenos Aires, in the famous "barrio del tambor", of which José Antonio Wilde speaks. I dare to say that his name is a Castilian word, derived from Latin: tangere.

It would not be strange, then, that some preacher of those who at that time sprinkled his speeches with latinises and based on the fact that this was the only dance in which couples linked, would have called it the dance of touching, that is, tango, from the Latin tangere, to touch.

The explanation is not wrong.

The refined and cultured tango was introduced in the halls, and, without losing its grace, it captured the sympathy of modern mothers. Of the old ones, do not say!

— The tango?

— What immorality! The most serious crime of which Manuelita Rosas is accused is that of her presence in the candombé, watching her dance the tango of the blacks.

In Carlos Ibarguren's book we see the poor girl witnessing, by order of her father, how black couples melted into tango.

She was bound by her parental policy.

The tyrant needed the blacks of Buenos Aires — thirty percent of the population — to believe in her protective affection.

He flattered them by sending them what she loved the most: her daughter... And let it be said that Manuelita herself, so as not to snub the black woman, also danced the primitive tango with them.

The great Restorer was not wrong.

Here is what José Antonio Wilde tells us:

« The blacks got to have their... black page. The time of Rosas came, which unhinged everything... In the espionage system established by the tyrant, the blacks entered to provide him with an important service, betraying several families and accusing them of unitary savages. »

The tango, then, contributed to the struggles of the tyranny.

After the black ladies became haughty and insolent, and the rich ladies came to fear them as much as the Mazorca.

The tango came out of the candombés to become enthroned in the old neighborhood of San Telmo, where the slaughterhouses were. Later, the tango went to Boca del Riachuelo, from where the accordion Genovese and the guitar, introduced in the criolla dance a more cult feeling of harmony, without the dance losing its voluptuous grace. Later, the bandoneon perfected its movements, giving it more education and purifying it from time to time. Then, the first written tango appeared, which was called "Bartolo", and from there the tango jumped onto the stage of national theatres, where Ezequiel Soria had Spanish artists such as Enrique Gil, Félix Mesa, Ángeles Montilla, Julio Ruiz dance it... Thus, tango embarked for Europe and prevailed in the theatres of Cadiz, Seville, Barcelona and Madrid... The "Bella Otero" emerged and took it to Paris, where Liana de Pougy fell in love with its rhythm, spread it like a barbaric dance among her Parisian songs, and, immediately, Mistinguett canonized it along with the Brazilian machicha. Such is the history of our beautiful tango. But, as there is no history without philosophy, here is where the national dance has its own.

— Dancing — Henri Bergson has said — is the philosophical law of movement.

It has between the sexes the same importance of the word. Sometimes a tango turn speaks more to a woman's soul than ten volumes of Shakespeare.

This opinion of the elegant philosopher of the Sorbonne is approved by the dance teacher Juan Eugenio de Chikoff himself, who affirms:

— Tango in the salons has brought as a consequence a social connection that did not exist in the past when the minuet, so beautiful and so mystical, kept men and women separated by a coldness that gave social gatherings the happy sadness of the wakes of little angels.

The aristocratic, artistic tango, which allows harmonious phrases to be made with the feet, extinguishes the fear that women usually inspire in men. This is the truth. The man, who thinks he is so audacious, so aggressive, so brave with women, feels so little in front of them, that only tango reminds him that he is the Dominator.

— Dancing — I don't know who said — is: At fifteen, an organic necessity. At twenty-five a moral necessity. At forty, a social necessity. At fifty, a philosophical necessity. At sixty, there is no longer a need.

As for tango, it will always continue to live in the ballrooms making drawings in the air, like butterflies. It is useless that other dances want to eclipse their dominance. Tango comes from Tangere; from "noli me tangere" (don't touch me). Tango seems, then, to say the same thing: — "noli me tangere" —, translated into the Argentine language: — ¡Nadie me pisa el poncho! (Nobody steps on my poncho!)

Article republished in the TANGO CLUB Magazine No. 48, March-April 2001

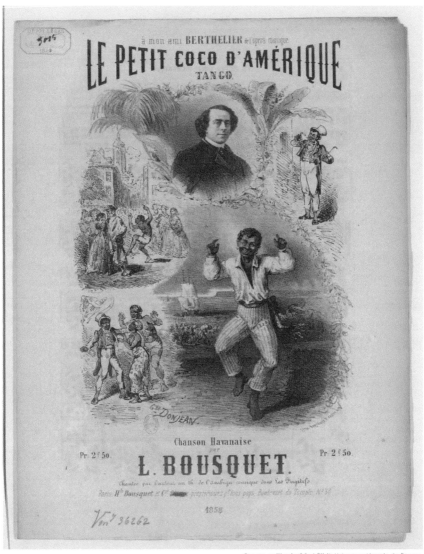

Figure 5: "Tango Habanera" – illustration "Le Petit Coco d' Amérique ou Tango, chanson havanaise" (1858) by Gustave Donjean (1800 - 1899), music by Louis Bousquet (18.. - 1899)

3 THE TANGO LESSON

Tango and Champagne usually they go well with each other. As in the case of Champagne which is a sparkling wine blended from other base wines of specific grapes like Pinot Noir, Pinot Meunier, Chardonnay, as in Tango which is a city dance blended from other folk dances. Teaching the Tango should follow metaphorically a similar approach of making Champagne, otherwise it will take years to master the Tango, instead of a few lessons.

In this sense we will present a Tango Lesson that will guide you to have a taster feeling experience of the authentic Tango in just 60 minutes:

I. The Tango Lesson's structure (60 min)
II. The Angolan vibe: Kizomba (15 min)
III. The Cuban vibe: Habanera (15 min)
IV. The Spanish vibe: Milonga (15 min)
V. The Argentinian vibe: Tango (15 min)

I. The Tango Lesson's structure (60 min)

"Dance is the mother of the arts. Music and poetry exist in time; Painting and architecture in space, but dance lives in space and time at the same time. The creator and the creation, the artist and the work are still one here. Rhythmic patterns of movement, plastic sense of space... this is what the human creates in dance in his own body before using matter, stone and words to express his inner experiences...." ~ Curt Sachs (1881 - 1959), author of the 'World History of the Dance' (1937)
https://archive.org/details/worldhistoryofda00sach/

This Tango Lesson was designed to help you feel and enjoy the Tango from the start. There will four modules of 15 minutes each, to help you to understand where the Tango comes from.

The first three modules are dances as Kizomba, Habanera and Milonga and the last module will be the Tango which will be a blend of the previous modules.

Like in the case of the Champagne where it is usually made from a blend of three grapes such as Pinot Noir, Pinot Meunier and Chardonnay.

Nevertheless, those three grapes used in the Champagne are not the only ones but the main ones of a group of seven authorized grapes.

Like in the case of the Tango where it was also blended with other folk dances such as candombé, flamenco, mazurka, tarantella and so forth. Likewise, in Champagne, not all the Champagne wines will taste the same, and so in the Tango is important that you could embedded your own personality as well. To help you on that achievement, each module will begin with an Energy exercise and will end with an Embrace exercise.

The last Embrace exercise will be done with a blindfold that will be the final proof that you can feel the tango dancing without any previous dancing experience whatsoever. In each module, the steps to be taught will fit on the music to be listen.

To guide you in your curiosity about what this Tango Lesson is all about, you could review the following supporting materials:
https://www.youtube.com/playlist?list=PLhuguMXj7ec5ttkYNscjDjsQ5TiZu2_kp

a)   ENERGY:
a.1) Music: Yoga "Queen Bee – Ajai Alai"
https://youtu.be/M2t1F0EIgUg
a.2) Exercise: Donna Eden's 5 min Energy Routine
https://youtu.be/akIlrF-HSJM
a.3) Tangomania film: "Max, Professeur de Tango" by Max Linder, 1912
https://youtu.be/SM7ioJJNUT4

c) KIZOMBA:
b.1) Music: Criola
https://youtu.be/ULtvfzHeCYA
b.2) Exercise: Kizomba 5 basic steps by João Capela Academy
https://youtu.be/8t0AoHicsCs
b.3) Tangomania book: "The Secrets of the Tango" by Samuel Chester, 1914 (with Tango instruction by the Argentinian Juan Barrasa)
https://blogs.harvard.edu/preserving/2011/03/09/it-takes-two-to-tango/

d) HABANERA:
c.1) Music: Habanera - "Carmen of Bizet"
https://youtu.be/gM_DsTTBB6k
c.2) Exercise: Habanera by Sanguineti Bosio
https://youtu.be/rCjw3VdnYSA
c.3) Tangomania book: "El Tango Argentino de Salón" by Nicanor Lima, 1916 (with Tango instruction by the Argentinian Nicanor Lima)
https://socialdance.stanford.edu/Syllabi/El_Tango_Argentino.htm

e) MILONGA:
d.1) Music: Tango "9 de Julio, 1916"
https://youtu.be/quOnaPGfWY0
d.2) Exercise: Early Paris Tango 1911-1913
https://youtu.be/r_TPZz4dybs
d.3) Tangomania book: "The guide to the Tango" by P.J.S Richardson, 1914 (with Tango instruction by the Argentinian Raoul de Alvez)
https://catalog.hathitrust.org/Record/100695400

e) TANGO:
e.1) Music: Tango "El 13"
https://youtu.be/Z_uEzQ-IHao
e.2) Exercise: Tango scenes from the film Tango Bar (1987)
https://youtu.be/wxGE0vPxmfI
e.3) Tangomania book: "The tango" by Maurice Mouvet, 1914 (with Tango instruction from Argentinean Benigno Macias at Maxim's in Paris)
https://www.loc.gov/resource/musdi.239.0?st=gallery

f) EMBRACE:
f.1) Music: Tango "El Choclo"
https://youtu.be/B21qn_dtPqc
f.2) Exercise: The Embrace at Buenos Aire, 70s
https://youtu.be/8xcCchEWtGU
f.3) Tangomania film: "Is dance in decline?" by Isaac Grünewald, 1915
https://www.filmarkivet.se/movies/ar-dansen-pa-forfall/

"Between 1865 and 1895, various musical traditions blended and eventually formed what would later be identified as tango. The habanera, the Andalusian tango, and the milonga— an Afro-Argentine form of popular dance related to candombé-all came to influence the early rhythmic development of the musical genre. In its early stages, the Argentine tango was mainly the dance and music of the urban poor, the socially unacceptable, and the disinherited of Buenos Aires's outskirts (working-class neighborhoods). In the dance academies and bordellos, young upper-class men joined the lower classes in their appreciation of the tango. Everybody seemed to find a source of satisfaction in its egalitarian embrace. For the upper classes, it was a means of escaping social restrictions. For the less fortunate, tango lyrics expressed the alienation of urban life, while the dance's sharply tangled steps provided a form of release." ~ Simon Collier in "The Birth of Tango"
https://youtu.be/8hu2IyKjif4

In truth, the Spanish Basque composer Sebastián Iradier y Salaverri (1809 – 1865) has been the father of the musical structure of the 2x4 Argentine Tango. "El Arreglito" is Iradier's best known piece, after the "La Paloma", a habanera composed by him, is firmly at the top of the charts and remains popular in Spain, Mexico and Germany. Both "El Arreglito" and "La Paloma" were composed by Iradier around 1860 after a visit to Havana, Cuba. "El Arreglito" has the characteristics of the Habanera as well, two-by-four compás and phrases with triplets and eights:
https://youtu.be/YFDurZPYTDU

"El Arreglito ou la Promesse de mariage", was a habanera used by Georges Bizet in his opera Carmen. Bizet, thinking it was a popular song, was inspired by the melody and recomposed it into the aria "L'amour est un oiseau rebelle", also known as "Bizet's Habanera". When he discovered his mistake, Bizet added a note to the opera's vocal score, acknowledging its origin to the composer Sebastian Iradier. In the piece "Carmen de Bizet", José is the only person on stage who does not pay attention to Carmen while she sings the Habanera, and after she finishes he approaches her, and at the end of the next short scene, after from Carmen's spoken words "épinglier de mon âme" and her throwing a cassia flower to José, the female chorus repeats the refrain:
« L'amour est enfant de bohème,
Il n'a jamais, jamais connu de loi,
Si tu ne m'aimes pas, je t'aime,
Si je t'aime, prends garde à toi ! »
The refrain also returns briefly at the end of the act, in scene XI, No. 1 Final where Carmen hums it in Lieutenant Zuniga's face.
https://youtu.be/KJ_HHRJf0xg

The Argentine maestro and pianist Mario Marzán explains to us in this video how Bizet's "Habanera" led to the famous tango "El Choclo": https://youtu.be/XQgWplQhbqQ

The first rhythm of the tango is taken from Cuba and is called the Habanera. These rhythms are used as the basis for both the bass line and the percussion parts. Although there are many variations, these two are the main rhythmic cells. Remember, tangos tend to be in either 4/4 or 2/4, and while there are some exceptions in other meters, this is considerably less common and makes it much harder to produce convincing results. Most tangos begin in a minor key, reflecting the serious nature of the dance (indeed, most dancers keep stern faces when dancing tangos). Melodies also tend to use lots of chromatic notes, so use these to fill in any gaps between tones in your melody. Rhythmically, melodies can move either with the bass line, or they can play flowing straight notes to contrast the dotted rhythms in the other instruments. Tangos use relatively simple harmony, which contrasts the more complicated rhythms and melodies. In most tangos, the harmony comes out through the bass line, or a through a piano accompaniment. https://composerfocus.com/how-to-write-a-tango/

The famous Argentinian pianist Horacio Salgán (1916 – 2016) described in his book "Curso de Tango" (Course of Tango) the initial influence of the Habanera in the Tango:

"Before getting into the matter, we must point out the difference between the Tango of the first period, with the accompaniment of Habanera, and the Tango in its most up-to-date conception, with the accompaniment that we commonly call "in four", to which was added the infinite variety of rhythmic figures that we know today. The difference between one and the other is such that at times it is difficult to establish – except for their melodies – a link between the two, due to the evolution and changes that have taken place in it. Let us see below some data regarding the rhythm of Habanera which, as we know, was the first accompaniment of Tango.

In the ANTHOLOGY OF RIOPLATENSE TANGO, excellent work carried out by the NATIONAL INSTITUTE OF MUSICOLOGY "CARLOS VEGA", we find the following information:

« Setting English Country-Dance as a starting point, we find it received with interest in France towards the end of the 17th century; It then passes to America, where it is documented already transformed into a Cuban contradanza in the 19th century. This produces two sub-species: one of them, the 2x4, gives rise to the Habanera...

The Habanera is taken to Europe and is widely accepted; the stylized version converted into a ballroom dance, reaches the Río de La Plata where it settles among the triumphant dances...

This complex back-and-forth process will occur repeatedly during the time that interests our analysis.

Alejo Carpentier, a well-known Cuban musicologist and writer, warned of this mechanism... »

It means then that, from the stylized Habanera of Europe, Tango takes its first form of accompaniment, reaching it perhaps through Andalusian Tango and/or Zarzuela music, since many worshipers of that genre were among the first authors of Tangos such as, for example, Don Feliciano Latasa – born in San Sebastián – composer of the Tango "Gran Hotel Victoria".

The accompaniment used in the early days of Tango comes from Andalusian Tango. Some possible influence is also attributed to the Milonga.

In short, the opinions are many and that is why, correctly, the ANTHOLOGY says:

« Dances – choreography and music – generally have a haphazard existence; they suffer stylistic changes, morphological adjustments, they change their name, they change their residence.

It is naive to try to determine a unilinear retrospective path that leads to the origins...

The history of the Contradanza that we have just observed can provide us with an example of these processes... »

The Habanera accompaniment remained in Tango for a not very long period. When the Tango comes to materialize in the musical genre that we know today, it abandons that rhythm, which only appears exceptionally. Already abandoned, the accompaniment of the Habanera, (which is written in 2x4), and when the Tango begins the rhythmic marking that we call "in four", numbering the compass of the same in 2x4 was continued. Then, considering that numbering in 2x4, when in reality 4 eighth notes were being marked, it was decided to relate the numbering of the compass to said marking and the 2x4 was replaced by the 4x8. Currently the writing of Tango is numbered in 4x4. This was done for reasons of convenience, since in the passages that contain figures of short duration, such as the variations, instead of using the sixteenth notes as was previously done, sixteenth notes are written, which allows a clearer and more precise writing. less laborious.

Now let's go to the essentials: the essential in this case is the sound, that is, how it sounds. Is there any difference in execution when we play a Tango written in 2x4, 4x8, or 4x4? None.

We speak obviously from the moment that the Habanera accompaniment was no longer used.

It should be noted that some authors use the figures (round, white, black, etc.), in the opposite direction to their traditional use.

Let us take Beethoven as an example, who wrote fast times such as: Scherzos in quarter notes (see 3rd and 7th Symphonies) and, instead, slow ones, in muses (see Sonata Largo No. 7, Op. 10 No. 3, for Piano).

This is explained, because the value of the figures depends on the indication with which the movement is headed, that is, if it is indicated as Allegro, Lento, Presto, etc.

In practice, listing 2x4, 4x8, or 4x4 in Tango has not altered or influenced its execution or its spirit." Horacio Salgán
https://www.amazon.co.uk/Horacio-Salg%C3%A1n-CURSO-TANGO/dp/9872882703

In the year 1913, the writer H.G. Wells (1866 - 1946) noted, was "the year of the tango." This new dance where couples danced cheek-to-cheek, legs and arms pressed close against each other in an erotic embrace, had everyone's attention.

"Don't you have to be lying down to dance that?" This, according to Gabriel-Louis Pringué (1885 - 1965), chronicler of Parisian high society in the first half of the twentieth century, was what Comtesse Mélanie de Portalès (1836 - 1914) whispered into the ear of the "distinguished academician" seated next to her, while they were both watching a couple learning to tango.

"The first concern of elegant women is to go and learn with a famous dance master" wrote Comtesse Éliane in L'Art et la Mode on 3 May 1913: "from the surrounding chateaus, they all go to Paris for their tango lesson." Thus, tango was "all the rage" and "the question which is asked in dances in the winter of 1912 to 1913" is "Do you tango?"
https://www.cairn-int.info/article-E_CLIO1_046_0087--dancing-with-le-sexe-eroticism-and.htm

"« Do you tango? » This is the question that arose at the balls this winter [1912 – 1913], first a timid fire, with a smile that excused the negative answer in advance, then in a more assured and confident tone. not admitting defeat, as if one were inquiring about the most natural thing in the world... It was therefore necessary to learn the tango, and everyone rushed enthusiastically to the lessons of the fashionable teachers, in order to receive good principles, there. Well-advised housewives have organized small meetings in their homes, where young men and girls are initiated into the choreographic secrets they are burning to know. And there are, in the evening, for the circle of friends who form the intimacy here, charming lessons, given by a lady expert in the art of teaching the difficult steps of which the new dance is composed, "el corte", "el paseo", "la media luna". Grouped around her, her students listen to her, follow her with their eyes, while others, to the sound of the tireless piano, try to apply the rules they have just learned... The Tango which is thus introduced into the Parisian salons has nothing of the Spanish

tango, whose name evokes the disordered "ferias". Argentinian in origin, hardly modified for having crossed the seas, it is presented as a march for two, with slow and flexible movements, very rhythmic by the music. Will the tango replace, in worldly favor, the double and triple "boston", as these were carried away on the waltz? For the moment, it is all the rage, and we do not find it more daring than its predecessors. But where are the dances of yesteryear? ..." ~ L'Illustration, page 275, 1913 March 29.
https://www.gutenberg.org/files/37874/37874-h/37874-h.htm

In Paris, one of the introducers of this dance was the Catalan José Sentís (1888 - 1983), who opened a dance academy in rue de la Faizanderie. Bernabe Simarra (1881 -?), Ricardo Guiraldes (1886-1927), who is known to have given tango exhibitions in Madame Rezké's salon, and Enrique Saborido (1878 – 1941) hired by Madama Rezké for her new Tango Academy in Paris.
http://hemerotecadigital.bne.es/issue.vm?id=0004677297&page=126

José Gobello (1919 – 2013), president (1995-2013) of the "Academia Porteña del Lunfardo", said that « even though it might seem a joke, Paris is the place from where the tango de salon came to Argentina »
http://hemerotecadigital.bne.es/issue.vm?id=0004677297&page=126

In Paris, one of the introducers of this dance was the Catalan José Sentís (1888 - 1983), who opened a dance academy in rue de la Faizanderie. Bernabé Simarra (1881 - ?), Ricardo Güiraldes (1886-1927), who is known to have given tango exhibitions in Madame Rezké's salon, and Enrique Saborido (1878 – 1941) hired by Madame Rezké for her new Tango Academy in Paris in 1913.

Little by little, many tango dancers, composers and singers would arrive in Europe, precisely because tango in Argentina, at least in its origins, was a dance native to the "conventillos", the suburban outskirts, a bohemian damp mould as it is not recognized as a manifestation of any art, but as a danger of moral contamination and the inevitable "idiotization" of the youth of Buenos Aires.

In order to safeguard the "purity" of the nation, tango had to find its maximum expression in the Paris of the Belle Époque, where this initial repudiation would end up becoming a symbol of elegance, refinement and artistic education. In this way, Paris became Tanguinópolis, and, where before there was only misery and vice, exasperation and stinginess, an atmosphere of gallant, restrained and worldly party had been created in the capital of the Seine.

Tango had begun to undergo transformations, according to the novelist from Madrid Agustín R. Bonnat, sometimes required by coquetry, other times by the perhaps sinful tendencies of the dances and, others by the demands of aesthetics and the environment required on stage. of art. With all these changes, the authenticity of "compadrón" tango ended up being distorted in a "vicious and cocky atmosphere of mask dances".

Now, as it was practiced, it was a slow, serious, elegant, distinguished, aristocratic, chaste and, above all, complicated dance, where the young ladies and "good girls" were counting the steps with extraordinary care, well, with the slightest mistake, the tango was spoiled. A whole compendium of norms and rules with which any young lady, if she learned them correctly, could win the unconditional sympathy of high society.

Before the Great War, for many young people, upstarts in night entertainment, the dance meant a cheerful caricature of a very particular way of being and living. The Valencian liberal newspaper, Eco de Levante, reported on the attitude that they took when externalizing their way of dancing on nights in the music-halls or the dances that their way of dancing was in fashion:

"[…] dancing drives them crazy, it makes them drunk much more than sipped champagne, and already thrown into full dance fever, they take off their hats, stick to a man, and with their faces flushed, their eyes cloudy, their hair gracefully in disorder, they please the body, until they fall exhausted, but not satisfied. These women –and all women in general– have dancing as a vice; they like it so much that for some, men are divided into two classes: those who dance and those who do not dance, and the former will always be preferred to the latter, until there is the strange case that women who go with their partner end the night with others who dance."

Alberto Insúa, a famous writer and then chronicler in Paris for the Madrid publication La Ilustracion Española y Americana, portrayed this reality by recounting the new greyish hue that the French capital had taken on during the Great War:

"The Paris fair has turned off its lights; There is no Argentine tango or Montmartresque orgies? … Many impure things, which were only guests of Paris, have emigrated by force. And at night, the majestic silhouettes of Our Lady, the Place de la Concorde and the Pantheon discover a new meaning, a hitherto unknown soul. They speak of serenity, firmness and faith… And while these conversations between the sacred stones and suffering men unfold in the shadows, what noise is this that arises from the bowels of Paris? What do those lights mean, that traffic that shakes a great artery of the capital? something prosaic"

To highlight the wink that Insúa makes to the reader when pointing out that Parisian cosmopolitanism is in a "fallen layer". Neither the light pollution, nor the orgiastic cocktail of drugs and sex, nor cursed dances like the Argentine tango, nor anything that could be "impure" continued to survive in Paris, because it had simply emigrated, supposedly beyond the Pyrenees. By fleeing all those elements that had given character to the Ville Lumière, the city had ended up losing its identity. Federico García Sanchiz,

New World correspondent in Paris, extolling the supremacy of Parisian women, both in beauty and in spirit, warned, well into the Great War, that the "Parisian fairies" had stopped dancing the tango. Apparently, according to the writer, the female heart in Paris had a softer, more winged rhythm and its palpitations had a greater "smell of worldliness." However, in these times, the hearts of Parisians could hardly beat with the same rhythm as it did during the Belle Époque.
https://lecturesdugenrefr.files.wordpress.com/2019/03/luengo_r6.pdf

Richard Powers, the Profesor of Historical Dance in the renowed Stanford University, made an extensive research of the tango steps being taught and danced in Europe during the Tangomania:
https://www.libraryofdance.org/dances/early-tango/
In a Historical Dance workshop dedicated to tango, Richard Powers made a demonstration of the figures being danced in Paris between 1911 and 1913:
https://youtu.be/r_TPZz4dybs

In 1913 the Tango Belt in New Orleans was named after the Tango craze that was sweeping the country. The Tango Belt spanned several blocks bound by St. Louis, Dauphine, Iberville and North Rampart. This was a place where both black and white patrons could enjoy music and dance.

Many clubs hosted jitney dances, where patrons paid to dance with women.

The Princess and the Frog is a 2009 American animated musical fantasy romantic comedy film produced by Walt Disney Animation Studios and released by Walt Disney Pictures.

The 49th Disney animated feature film, it is loosely based on the 2002 novel The Frog Princess by E. D. Baker, which in turn is based on the German folk tale "The Frog Prince" as collected by the Brothers Grimm.

Set in New Orleans during the 1920's, the film tells the story of a hardworking waitress named Tiana who dreams of opening her own restaurant.

After kissing a prince who has been turned into a frog by an evil witch doctor, Tiana becomes a frog herself and must find a way to turn back into a human before it is too late.

Making their home in the Tango Belt, it makes sense that Princess Tiana and Prince Naveen would perform the Tango, the dance of Love, for their first dance.

Not far from the French quarter they would have had access to the French Tango.

A passionate beginning to these star-crossed amphibians.
https://www.adventuresindance.com/2020/03/tianas-french-tango-dance-how-to/

"« To think, » Prince Naveen murmurs, his lips pressed to the curve of her throat, « that you claimed you couldn't dance! »

Princess Tiana smiles, her hands in his hair, leaning back to catch his eye. « In case you haven't noticed, sugar, right now we're not dancing. »

She arches her spine pointedly, and he groans for the movement, for the way she tightens around him, so slick and heated.

« And yet we are, » he replies with a wink, his hand at the base of her spine, tipping her backward slightly.

Her legs tighten around his waist, feeling so full and content with him inside of her, like she could stay like this forever. Except she's maybe growing a little impatient, wanting that sweet release he's so good at giving her. He pulls her back up, and Tiana wraps her arms around his neck, pressed chest to chest, spread across his lap.

« Believe me, » he purrs, voice deep and husky. « You have a natural rhythm. »

Tiana laughs and, oh, that does wonderful things to her insides when he's got her all wound up like this.

« Well, my 'natural rhythm' would like to move things along a bit faster, if you don't mind. »

Naveen grins, flashing bright white teeth that feel so good when they nibble at her ears. He's sweating, flushed, hair tousled and gorgeous, and his hands grip her hips, raise her up and pull her down, just how she likes it. Tiana moans, bracing her feet against the mattress, riding every thrust of his hips, fingernails dragging lightly down the back of his neck to make him shiver.

« The way you move, » he sighs, awed by her, and she feels beautiful and alive in his arms. Holding him close, clenching down around him, pleasure building higher and higher into that bright peak of sensation. Maybe he's right, maybe this is dancing, because she swears, she can hear music in the way their hearts beat in perfect time."
https://1drabble.livejournal.com/150431.html

The king of the "French Tango" (known as Tango de Salon in Buenos Aires) of the Hollywood movies has been the famous North American actor George Raft who learned Tango on his trip to Paris as he told in this video:
https://youtu.be/Wo48DgJFPUE

One of George Raft's most famous scenes is « Do you tango? » dancing with Coleen Gray in the movie "Lucky Nick Cain" in 1951:
https://youtu.be/8WDYPw-IkeE

Georges Raft has also danced the Argentine Tango that was danced in London in 1913, as a "taxi dancer" in the movie "Bolero" in 1934:
https://youtu.be/x7F8I4tulOk

Likewise, the French dancers invented the denomination "Tango Argentin" to distinguish from the Spanish Tango of the XIX century, the British dancers invented the denomination of "French Tango" for the style Tango de Salón that was being newly developed in the Cabarets of Paris in the 1920's. The Argentinians never used the term "Argentine Tango" to describe its own tango, they just say "El Tango", as well the French never used the term "French Tango" to describe its own tango, they just say "Le Tangó". The Argentinian press was very confused with the new trend after the WWI and they published an article to show their discontentment, in the Argentinian magazine "Mundo Argentino", on December 25, 1929:

"'"El Tango" and… "Le Tangó"
Now it turns out that our shaken national tango is being modified by the good French and the no less excellent sons of the "blond Albion" [the British]. The dance teachers of those countries have created steps, turns, beats and even dips with which our tango acquired fox-trot and shimmy contours. The photographs that illustrate this page reproduce the demonstrations that a well-known English dancer, Victor Silvester, gave a few weeks ago at the Savoy Hotel in London, where he successfully rehearsed his new choreographic creations in five steps (the backward cut, the step forward, the walk, the sidestep and turns) to the obvious detriment of the Argentine tango. In Europe these involuntary detractors of our national tango abound, who make tango a completely arbitrary dance."
https://digital.iai.spk-berlin.de/viewer/image/840581548/5

Victor Silvester (1900 – 1978) was an English dancer, writer, musician and bandleader from the British dance band era. He was a significant figure in the development of ballroom dance during the first half of the 20th century, and his records sold 75 million copies from the 1930s through to the 1980s. He was one of the first post-war English dancers to feature the full natural turn in the slow waltz. This innovation was a factor in his winning the first World Ballroom Dancing Championship in 1922 with Phyllis Clarke as his partner. He married Dorothy Newton a few days later.

There are two videos where Victor Silvester is dancing the tango filmed by British Pathé:
1 – Silvester's tango dancing with his wife Dorothy Newton
https://youtu.be/bmfMhFaKJOM
2 – Silvester's tango dancing with his dance partner Phyllis Clarke
https://youtu.be/q-oa-Xu2F9Y

Nevertheless the "father" of this "New Tango" post-WWI or "French Tango" which was later known in Buenos Aires as "Tango de Salón", was the famous actor and tango dancer Rudolph Valentino (1895 – 1926).

Rudolph Valentino wrote a few instructional tango articles about this style for the American magazine "SCREENLAND" in 1922:

1 – Valentino's tango article with the actress Agnes Ayres

"THE NEW TANGO

The tempo and movement of the tango is slower than that of the popular ballroom dances. The music of the tango has the appeal of the waltz, because it reaches one's sense of rhythm and love for harmony. A good tango dancer must abandon himself to the cadence of the music to do the dance well. Like in a waltz, mechanical perfection does not make one a good dancer. In this group of pictures of Miss Ayres and myself all the steps of this fascinating dance are shown. In trying to master the figures, remember that the tango consists of steps forward similar to the fox-trot, which are followed by the side-steps." ~ Rudolph Valentino

http://www.noelledewinterdesign.com/agnesayresweb/agnesrudolphtango.htm

2 – Valentino's tango article with the actress Gloria Swanson

"HOW DO YOU DANCE?

Tango dancing is like acting. The better it is done the easier it looks. You will wonder when you begin how anyone can learn it. After you know the tango, you will wonder why everyone can't do it. Last month Miss Swanson and I showed "Screenland" readers the importance of starting right by posing in incorrect dance postures. So now we are showing you the correct way to hold a partner in the tango. Do not become impatient and expect to learn the entire dance, with its maze of intricate steps, from one lesson. If twenty photographs, showing every figure in the dance, were shown to you at once, you would not learn to tango without absorbing each explanation, step by step. So, this month's "lesson" is devoted to the proper tango position and the first three steps. In next month's Screenland, the advanced figures of the dance will appear. And, also, I have asked the Editor to publish a fragment of tango music for the piano, which will be a great help to beginners in practicing the steps. After next month, you may not be a finished tango dancer, but you will have enough figures at your command to adapt to your use." ~ Rudolph Valentino

https://rudolphvalentino.tumblr.com/search/Tango

Rodolfo Pietro Filiberto Raffaello Guglielmi di Valentina d'Antonguolla (1895 – 1926), known professionally as Rudolph Valentino and nicknamed "The Latin Lover", was an Italian actor based in the United States. In 1913, after finishing his high-school in Italy, Valentino visited Paris where he learned the tango from the rich playboy Argentinians who were dancing the tango in the famous restaurant Maxim's of Paris. At the end of 1913, Valentino travelled to New York where he became a tango teacher in the famous restaurant Maxim's of New York until 1915. In that period of time Valentino also met the famous Argentino tango dancer Casimiro Ain who

was establishing a Tango Academy in New York. Due to a love affair with his tango student, a rich married lady, he had to escape to the other side of USA and arrived at Hollywood where he finally became a worldwide film star and being known as the "World's Greatest Tango Dancer". In Hollywood he made a scene of Spanish Tango in the movie "Blood and Sand" which was the first movie of Valentino that arrived at Japan:
https://youtu.be/TlqOLQ5OaNA

The most known tango scene of Valentino is the gaucho Argentine Tango scene being danced with the Spanish actress Beatriz Dominguez in the movie "The Four Horsemen of Apocalypse", a scene that he replicated later with his second wife (1923-1925), Natacha Rambova, in the famous Mineralava Tour of 1923 across USA:
https://youtu.be/C2_xWSrmko0

But the most underrated tango scene of Valentino is the gallant Parisian Tango scene being danced with the American actress Alice Terry in the same movie "The Four Horsemen of Apocalypse", a scene that later helped to revive the Tango de Salon in the Cabarets of Paris in the decade of the 1920's:
https://youtu.be/OWyIpc6D5eE

After finishing those two movies, Valentino returned to Europe around 1922 and visit the Cabaret "El Garrón" (former "Princesse" before WWI) which was being managed by the famous Argentinian bandoneonist Manuel Pizarro. As legend has it, the star of the silent screen, Rudolph Valentino, accompanied by his first wife (1919-1923), Jean Acker, were in the audience. Manuel Pizarro asked if they would be obliged to demonstrate the Tango. Valentino readily accepted and danced with his companion to "El Choclo", the unforgettable composition by Angel Villoldo. They may not have strictly followed the true Argentine steps, but nevertheless offered an elegant, Hollywood-style version of the dance. Following in their footsteps, the other punters all rushed to the dance floor, daring to dance themselves. Manuel Pizarro had won - from this moment onwards, Tango became a dance in Paris. The success was enormous and "El Garrón", along with "Le Palermo" on the ground floor of the same building attracted the throngs and were appreciated as Tango's Parisian headquarters for decades.
https://www.fremeaux.com/en/2502-manuel-pizarro-3561302501925-fa5019.html#livret

The concepts of the Parisian Cabarets "El Garrón" and "Le Lido" were exported to Buenos Aires by the French businessman Charles Seguin who opened in Buenos Aires the most famous Cabaret "Chantecler" (1924-1960). Its design fitted the purpose, the entrance allowed for cars to park and leave the attendants directly on the footsteps of the building, while being received by the buttons. The inside of Chantecler portrayed three dance floors, an enormous stage, red velvet curtains covering the balcony where you could directly order by phone what you wished to consume. At the back, the place

had an exotic inside pool that gathered young and attractive women that entertained the guests while playing in the pool. This cabaret used to be a meeting point for various artists, politicians, tourists and wealthy people that would enjoy drinking, eating, watching the shows (most of them were tango based) of popular artists as Carlos Gardel, José Razzano, Leguisamo, Celedonio Flores, Cadícamo. By the 1930's, the famous Argentinian Tango Orchestra bandleader Juan D´Arienzo he performed daily, every night and where he got the nicknamed of "El Rey del Compás". And by 1933, when Argentina Sono Films made its first movie "Tango!", Juan D'Arienzo was hired to participate in the movie's orchestra, performing in the "Chantecler", where he played the violin exquisitely at the rhythm of the tango "Chirusa", as seen in this video:
https://youtu.be/X5Ipk5oQsgw

From the Parisian Cabaret "El Garrón" the tango was again re-exported to Japan by the Japanese Baron Tsunayoshi Megata (1896 – 1969). In 1920 the Baron Megata went to Paris to undergo a surgical operation. He remained in the City of Lights until 1926, where he learned and mastered the art of dancing tango while patronizing in the cabaret "El Garrón". The Baron Megata later opened a tango academy in Tokyo to teach to the Japanese aristocracy free of charge how to dance the tango. He also published a book entitled "A method to dance the Argentine Tango" (Argentine Tango in the style of Tango de Salon or French Tango).

As a tribute to Baron Megata, a beautiful tango dancing scene was filmed between the Japanese actors Osamu Takizawa and Setsuko Hara in the Japanese film "The Ball at the Anjō House" of 1947, as seen in this video:
https://youtu.be/uJbXWb42MNw

Luis Alfredo Alposta, an Argentine physician, was the first person to reference the work of Megata as a pioneer in popularizing the tango in Japan. Alposta wrote the lyrics of "A lo Megata" ("The Megata Way") with music composed by Edmundo Rivero, as seen in this video:
https://youtu.be/Ko2w2-6mYtQ

"There are likewise three kinds of dancers:
First, those who consider dancing as a sort of gymnastic drill, made up of impersonal and graceful arabesques. Second, those who, by concentrating their minds, lead the body into the rhythm of a desired emotion, expressing a remembered feeling or experience. And finally, there are those who convert the body into a luminous fluidity, surrendering it to the inspiration of the soul." ~ Angela Isadora Duncan (1878 – 1927) was an American dancer who performed to great acclaim throughout Europe, US and Argentina.
https://youtu.be/AdyC6_s3S14

II. The Angolan vibe: Kizomba (15 min)

Energy (3 min): exercise "Hara-Line" (grounding)
Step (3 min): base 1 (double time)
Figure (3 min): base 2 (side step)
Sequence (3 min): base 3 (walk step)
Embrace (3 min): game "Balloon-chest" (hugging)

Kizomba is a great dance to practice dancing on the Beat.

Beat has a multitude of meanings, but typically it refers to the rhythmic and percussive elements of a song. If you have ever beatboxed to try to show someone how a song feels, you've displayed the beat to a person. The beat is often found in the way that the kick and snare of a drum or percussion set interact with the rhythm and tempo of a song. It is the most important and memorable percussive element of a song, and it can often be a distinguishing factor from other pieces of music. The beat is a very important thing to focus on when creating percussion-heavy songs. If you want to get people on their feet and dancing because of your song, focusing on creating a grooving and catchy beat will do that. The beat is the element that gives a song its danceability or lack thereof. The beat can also be decided based on the genre of music that is being created. If it is a song that is meant to be played in clubs and other places where hype is incredibly important, a steady quarter note beat might be exactly what the song needs. This is one of the simplest beats available but is still one of the best out there. In other musical genres using more complex beats can be helpful, but within the right context can make a song sound exciting and fresh to anyone who listens to it.

https://youtube.com/playlist?list=PLhuguMXj7ec4naP0MO6sGusAKuOnIDFDT

Why Tango?

"My dear Argentine friends who learned to dance in the Golden Age might raise an eyebrow to hear me say that. They would prefer to say, "Improvisando", where I might say, "A meditation performed by two who become one, united at the heart, seeking stillness through motion". They would say, "Manteniendo la relación entre los dos cuerpos" (maintaining the relationship between the two bodies), where I would say, "Keeping the hearts perfectly united at all times". But they would also say, quietly, so as not to be overheard and perhaps misunderstood, that dancing Tango is like being in love for three minutes." ~ Christine Denniston, writer of 'The Meaning of Tango' (2007)

Book: https://www.amazon.com/Meaning-Tango-Story-Argentinian-Dance-ebook/dp/B00QMJ5206/

Lesson: https://youtu.be/rdaVVDfIRpM

III. The Cuban vibe: Habanera (15 min)

Energy (3 min): exercise "Flex-Knees" (bending)
Step (3 min): El Paseo (walk)
Figure (3 min): El Corte (sway)
Sequence (3 min): La Media Luna (clock tic-tac)
Embrace (3 min): game "Life-belt" (listening)

Habanera is a great dance to practice dancing in the Tempo.

Tempo is the element of a song that decides how fast or slow a song's rhythm will feel.

Typically, it's very easy to tell when a song is slow or fast, even if a person isn't looking at the actual song's notation or production. Generally, people can tell how fast a song is just by listening to how it affects them.

Faster music is typically perceived as more energetic and exciting, while slower music usually feels more laid back and calm. This isn't always the case, but in most genres of music, the tempo of the music helps create the feeling of the song.

To establish a consistent tempo in a song, many producers and musicians will record their songs to a metronome, or a click track. This is a tool that sets a steady tempo for musicians to listen to as they record music so that the whole song can be the same tempo without any major shifts. However, many musicians actually appreciate the tempo shifts that come along with not recovering to a click.

Due to the energy level changing due to a faster or slower tempo, many artists will speed up in more energetic parts of a song and slowdown in less energetic parts of a song. This natural tempo change is very appealing to some musicians, depending on the style of music they are creating.

https://youtube.com/playlist?list=PLhuguMXj7ec6J03y6JJSEbbL7GJ3rLCLE

Why Tango matters?

"Some aged critics of the tango say they cannot see what happiness there is in dancing. Of course not! Folk don't dance to see; they dance to feel. Happiness is a choice of feeling, a thrilling, tingling harmony of mind and body, not an eyesight test! The only way of seeing the happiness that comes from the dance is to watch the smiling, radiant faces of the dancers. But for the true proof, try dancing." ~ Santos Casani, writer of 'Casani's Home Teacher - Ballroom Dancing Made Easy' (1930)

Book: https://www.amazon.co.uk/Casanis-Home-Teacher-Ballroom-Dancing/dp/1445513374
Lesson: https://youtu.be/4jE_ngF_UX0

IV. The Spanish vibe: Milonga (15 min)

Energy (3 min): exercise "Three-Thumps" (activating)
Step (3 min): La Cruz (the cross)
Figure (3 min): La Tijera (the scissor)
Sequence (3 min): El Ocho (the eight/the fan)
Embrace (3 min): game "Ribs-band" (dialoguing)

Milonga is a great dance to practice dancing to the Rhythm.

Rhythm is the element of music that makes the song have motion and flow. Songs will rest on the rhythm as they move forward and follow it throughout the song.

Rhythm is chiefly concerned with the element of time and the amount of noise and silence that different notes will have. Fundamentally speaking, music can't occur without time; the use of sound within the boundaries of time is what makes music, music.

Rhythm is the guide for a song and the glue that holds all of the different elements of a song together. Rhythm is often conveyed in a song through percussion and drums. That's because these are the elements that are most chiefly concerned with making sure the different elements of a song are working together. In the same way that drums will create a steady pulse for listeners to enjoy, these percussive elements ensure that the different musical instruments are all working together and not stepping on each other's toes.

https://youtube.com/playlist?list=PLhuguMXj7ec4UWI5VA6N7i4uYtF0MNtOJ

Why has Tango mattered in 1913?

"Many people who are taking up the Tango after not having danced for years delight in it for most unexpected reasons. Businessmen, especially, who suffer from systematic overwork, find the close attention it requires to master and carry out the many steps and figures a splendid antidote for brain-fag and business worries after a trying day, distracting the mind with even more complete success than bridge - of which, by the way, we seem to hear nothing nowadays, since the Tango craze came in-while providing exercise in pleasant company. Then the "Butterflies" and "Nuts" of Society find in Tangoing just that light occupation for the brain which they enjoy; and the modern woman suffering from "nerves" declares that in the dreamy, restful cadences and languorous movements of the Tango just the soothing qualities which she requires are to be found." ~ Gladys Beattie Crozier, writer of 'The Tango and How to Dance It' (1913)

Book: https://www.libraryofdance.org/manuals/1913-Crozier-Tango_(Powers).pdf
Lesson: https://youtu.be/x7F8I4tulOk

V. The Argentinian vibe: Tango (15 min)

Energy (3 min): exercise "Cross-Crawl" (powering)
Step (3 min): Ocho Milonguero (Ocho Cortado)
Figure (3 min): Ocho Tanguero (Ocho Planeo)
Sequence (3 min): Ocho Criollero (Ocho Boleo)
Embrace (3 min): game "Blindfold" (feeling)
https://www.youtube.com/playlist?list=PLhuguMXj7ec5ttkYNscjDjsQ5TiZu2_kp

Tango is a great dance to practice dancing by the Melody.

Melody is generally the part of a song that most people remember the most, because it is usually the element of a song that stands out the most.

The melody can be done by a singer singing lyrics, a guitar playing a lead line, or a soulful line of piano notes. These are parts of a song that can be as simple or complicated as the producer or songwriter wants.

Melody is the part of the music that is meant to communicate the main emotions of the song through musical terms. Often, the melody will carry the emotional weight of the song, even if the lyrics can't. Most good writers of melodies can tell the story of a song through the melody.

The melody will tell the listener if the song is sad, happy, angry, or anywhere in between.

Renowned songwriter Jeff Tweedy says that "The melody does the heavy lifting emotionally for a song." Understanding this fact can help inspire songwriters to create words that deeply match the melody, not the other way around.

The melody is almost always going to be the most memorable part of a song, so make sure to spend lots of time finding the right one when producing a song.
https://youtube.com/playlist?list=PLhuguMXj7ec5hvuSsBDrlbDq3Gj560HJA

Why Tango still matters?

"I believe that Tango has the potential to bring out the best in each of us, at least while in the embrace. We surrender our egos; leave prickly personality traits at the table; and cease to be CEOs, taxi drivers, engineers, unemployed. We replace all our externals with a purity of spirit, a generosity of kindness and splendid caring." ~ Johanna Siegmann, writer of 'The Tao of Tango' (2006)
Book: https://www.amazon.com/Tao-Tango-Johanna-Siegmann/dp/155212410X
Lesson: https://youtu.be/Ljs09BmehkM

Figure 6: "La Leçon de Tango", illustration by José Simont, magazine, L'Illustration, page 275, Paris, 1913 March 29

4 THE TANGO SECRET

The famous Argentine short-story writer, essayist, poet and translator, Jorge Luis Borges (1899 – 1986), once said that "the Tango can be discussed, and we discuss it, but it contains, like everything true, a secret".

For many people "the secret of the Tango" is quite similar to the secret of "the Law of Attraction" revealed by Rhonda Byrne and it will always depend in your belief system. But for many of us, the secret of the Tango is like a chemical reaction, a cocktail of unexplained emotions from goosebumps to blushing and other body feelings usually triggered when a human is in love:

I. The Tangoing, the embrace of the bodies

II. The Tangasm, the T-Spot of the Tango

III. The secrets of the Tango Milonguero in Buenos Aires

IV. The secrets of the Tango de Salon in Buenos Aires

V. The secrets of the Tango Criollo in Buenos Aires

I. The Tangoing, the embrace of the bodies

"It is not enough to have the most melodious voice to sing a tango. You have to feel it too. You have to live its spirit." ~ Carlos Gardel (1890 - 1935) https://youtu.be/aSKgufjTJuk

"Desire", the possibility of "rubbing" up against each other under the pretense of giving way to the dancing fashion of the time and the "flexibility" of body movements required by dancing the tango thus pushed female fashion to evolve.

These elements were, paradoxically, both more permitted and more suspicious as they relied on an "import" of uncertain and possibly doubtful origin, requiring caution and being as likely to legitimate or on the contrary to condemn the Parisian appropriation of this "carefree and exquisite [dance] from faraway countries, a dance that non-believers decry as immodest or grotesque".

Georges Goursat (aka Sem), who did not like this "neurosis," wrote that it had "made terrible progress":

« [...] through a lightning advance, it has spread across Paris, invading salons, theatres, bars, night clubs, large hotels and dance halls [...]
Half of Paris rubs up against the other half.
The entire town has been shaken up and has tango under its skin. »

In this context, debate emerged between opponents and defenders of tango, principally around the excessively sensual, even sexual, emphasis of this dance from elsewhere.

Thus, questions about that "elsewhere", about the origins of tango, a dance emerging from a doubly foreign place – geographically and socially distant – were connected to the apparently licentious properties attributed to the dance.

Analysis must begin by examining the choreography of tango, and particularly one of its fundamental features, that is to say the transition from the couple simply holding one another to being intertwined.

The words of Sem in the above quotation reveal this concern with the unambiguous connotations of the verb "rub" [frotter in French].

The male partner's forward-marching steps, and the systematic introduction of suspensions which interrupt the movement and make room for ornamental figures, sum up the innovative elements that tango brought to partner dancing.

These three aspects are interdependent according to Carlos Vega's analysis and technically they involve each other.

In the tango, the rejection of "perpetual motion" – i.e., sequential uninterrupted rhythmic or turning steps performed by the couple – is combined with sudden halts when either the woman or the man inserts improvised steps, whilst the partner stops completely: the result is to eliminate any regularity.

Prediction is impossible because the next dance move, the complete series, or even the entire theme are elaborated simultaneously as they are performed.

One technique becomes necessary: the couple must remain constantly intertwined. In other words, "the dancers have the following dilemma: either we hold on to each other, or we step on each other's feet".

In Paris, the disappearance of the distance between partners, the fact that there was no more "daylight" between partners, and the physical contact – of the chest or even the abdomen – was not seen as a technical necessity, but as an expression of lewdness.

Those in France or Europe who criticized or opposed the adoption of tango denounced its practices and the tastes that it displayed, which they saw as at best naive, but more often complacent, troubling and decadent. Thus, it was possible to describe this "pseudo-dance which must be criticized" as "a double belly-dance whose lewdness is increased by exaggerated contortions".

Some critics, like Sem, could therefore moralistically mock these "confusing sequences which have neither dance's momentum, nor its physical joy or delirium of movement". Swept up by the "drunkenness" and the "madness" of tango, people who are "excessively refined, saturated by luxury and comfort, used to the Ritz and the grand hotels" thus "rub up against each other" and "paw each other so obstinately and methodically" that you would believe them "to be practicing abdominal massage". It is neither a "therapy" nor a "physical exercise", but "a way of being sensual", more "a vice" than a "sport" about which it was impossible to say whether those who practiced it were "neurotics, exhibitionists or maniacs." As Sem noted, "faced with these mysterious and lascivious contortions", he felt "ill at ease, as if the hidden gestures of love were brusquely unveiled in public".

The press provides very abundant and useful descriptions, like the one given by "Parisiana" in L'Art et la Mode of 3 May 1913:

"Dancing on tiptoe, [the dancers] observe a harmonious silence, legs bent, proceeding without jolting, with a serene tranquility; they give the impression of people relaxing, but whose relaxation contains something of a radiance, the polish of a work of art. [...] Some have criticized the tango for being a dance that reduces people instead of elevating them, but one needs to see that it is an essentially modern entertainment, for those who, in their melancholy, have abdicated all hope."

"The first chords sound.

Lost sight as looking beyond what surrounds you.

Ears wide open so that the music enters and expands throughout your being.

A few seconds to merge with the body of your partner.

What foot is she standing on? Does she feel comfortable?

There are no words, it is a language of bodies, of perceptions.

In that moment of held breath, everything is expectation waiting for each note, each silence, each phrasing.

Your heart begins to beat in another way, as if seeking to be in tune with the heart of another being, feelings and sensations on the surface.

A barely perceptible deep breath, a slight flexion of the knees in a feline attitude preparing for its next movement, plus the position of the torso anticipates the action and the direction of the imaginary figures that, to the rhythm of the music and with fluidity, you will draw together with your partner, on the dance floor, like brushstrokes on a blank canvas, always considering the presence of other couples and the space, sometimes large and other times very small, to create.

By then you are already in a trance, you are already in another world, a world where everything is perfect or almost perfect, intimacy, listening, rhythm, time, setback, flow, play, waiting, balance, a world where there is no mistake." ~ Luis Silva, Buenos Aires, 2022
https://youtu.be/1F8ZYJYRQJ4

II. The Tangasm, the T-Spot of the Tango

"Tango has a way that we call it close embrace. The body doesn't think; the body feels the music as a way to move and walk, and if we put our attention to what our body is feeling, we will see that we are moving.

We only need to walk with elegance, transmitting to our partner in the embrace the energy we have from our chest (the heart chakra or energy zone of the body).

If you do it in this way can you transmit your energy to your partner. Improve each step and you will have the cadence of your own style." ~ Ricardo Vidort (1929 - 2006)
https://youtu.be/I3AJKXydkrI

What is the T-Spot of the Tango?

The embrace of the tango has five contact points: the cheek-to-cheek, the torso-to-torso, the solar plexus-to-solar plexus, the hand-to-hand and the hand on the back of each other.

The T-Spot is located in the front of the sternum, in the center of the torso, 6-8 millimeters deep in the subcutis and appears as a thickening of sensory nerve tissue: these are neurotransmitters for the perception of sensations such as pressure and rubbing.

Intense and ephemeral, Tangasm is present. Or not?

Tangasm is the search for the perfect embrace:

"A rare sensation experienced by two dancers in an exceptional complicity that plunges them into a state close to trance."

Tangasm is the only orgasm that lasts three minutes ... it is a sensation that completely invades you, vital, happy, that makes you feel floating in a wonderful dimension.

Tangasm is a second state in which the couple, for three minutes, is outside of time and space.

An ecstasy in which there is only her, him and the music.

It is when the tango is much more than a dance but a communion.

The milonga, with the other surrounding couples, no longer exists. The moist heat of the bodies has disappeared.

The light becomes a blurred background, the walls delimiting the track seem to have been pushed to the horizon.

There is only this bubble which is transported beyond the music.

The tempo seems to have suspended itself in an ether, the melody is a breath coming from who knows where.

There are no more steps or figures.

There is only one couple whose bodies are in perfect communion.

It lasts the time of a tango.

Then there is the exhalation, a few seconds after the final note.

The couple slowly get used to the earthly attraction from which they had freed themselves.

The embrace opens and the couple exchange a look of enjoyment.

A Tangasm occurs when the milonga energy is successfully exchanged.

This exchange causes a favorable cycle of responses, with the production of endorphins, acetylcholine and oxytocin, which lead to a complete harmony in the couple and, in this way, the chemistry of both will reach in a few moments the level of the true and purest Tangasm.

Each male dancer and each female dancer have a certain number of transmitters and receivers for tangasmic energy.

However, not all transmitters work with all receivers.

Slow tango helps to find true pleasure and to experience the dance better with your partner.

In fact, daily life is already too overwhelming, lived with fast and anxious rhythms and this harms the activity in the milongas.

You have to stop and spend more time with the person you are dancing with, not only to follow the rhythm, but also to understand the problems and concerns of everyday life.

Waiting for you to go to the kiosk or you don't want to buy these manuals, I recommend that you follow these ten simple tips.

Sure, they won't change your life, but they just might help you find or discover true joy on the dance floor:

a) Breathing slowly and deeply will help you relax.
b) Make sounds to express what they feel inside.
c) Pay attention to your body in order to really discover the pleasures of tango.
d) It is forbidden to follow precise patterns, it is better to move freely, in this way the dance will be much more captivating and exciting.
e) Pace does not mean speed.
f) Your goal is pleasure, not a challenge to satisfy your partner.
g) It is important to dedicate time to rapport with your partner before starting the tango.
h) h) Look for a milonga with the right atmosphere, with candles on the tables and adequate lighting.
i) Look for the ideal milonga for you, with relaxing objects and furniture.
j) Avoid awkward positions.

https://youtu.be/YIqoK4IlL-g

The biology behind the Tangasm

The thymus-spleen connection is an excellent technique for increasing energy that will be used as an exercise in the tango lesson of the previous chapter.

The Timo technique is widely used in many branches of Kinesiology, but if someone popularized it, it was its creator, the psychiatrist and kinesiologist Dr. John Diamond MD. This famous gland is located just above the chest, above the heart and below the thyroid, just behind the top of the breastbone. Physiologically, the function of the thymus is essential for the immune system; It is related to the production of white blood cells, specifically lymphocytes, so its function is closely related to protecting us against bacteria and viruses.

In the East, this gland is related to the heart chakra, and it is said that when this gland is activated again, it helps us access higher states of consciousness.

It is also curious that the Romans called the same plant that was used for infections and to stimulate the immune system, which was THYME in Latin or thymus.

The immune system is related to all the systems of the body, apparently it has nothing to do with the processes of the mind. However, science has been making progress in unraveling this complex body-mind relationship.

When our immune system is strong, we feel cheerful, happy or in love and we will hardly fall ill; however, negative emotions make us easily vulnerable to infections.

— How to stimulate our emotional escape valve?

Scientists have known for a long time that by stimulating the vagus nerve, we can improve our cognitive abilities and behavior and that it will also allow us to take advantage of its potential to remain calm in a tense moment.

It is the tenth of the cranial nerves, often called the "Nerve of Compassion", because when it is active, it helps create the "warm waves" that we feel in our chest when we are hugged or touched by something...

In the year 1921 the German physiologist named Otto Loewi discovered that the stimulation of the vagus nerve caused a reduction in the heart rate by releasing a substance that he called "Vagusstoff" in German, "Vagus substance".

The "vague substance" was later identified as acetylcholine and became the first neurotransmitter identified by scientists.

Vagusstoff is literally a natural tranquilizer that we can self-administer simply by taking a few deep breaths with long exhalations.

—   What is the Vagus Nerve?

The word vagus means "wanderer" in Latin. The vagus nerve is known as the wandering nerve as it has several branches that diverge into two thick stalks rooted in the cerebellum and brainstem that wander to the lower viscera of the abdomen touching the heart and most of the major organs in the abdomen. the way. The vagus nerve is constantly sending sensory information about the state of the organs to the brain. In fact, between 80 and 90% of the nerve fibers of the vagus nerve are dedicated to the communication of the state of the viscera to the brain. The vagus nerve is a bundle of nerves that originates from the top of the spinal cord. It activates different organs throughout the body (such as the heart, lungs, liver, and digestive organs). When activated, it can produce that warm expanding feeling in the chest, for example when we are touched by someone's kindness or when we appreciate a beautiful piece of music.

Neurologist Stephen W. Porges of the University of Illinois at Chicago argued long ago that the vagus nerve is the nerve of compassion, of course it serves many other functions as well. There are several reasons that justify this statement. The vagus nerve is believed to stimulate certain muscles in the vocal cavity, allowing communication. Reduces heart rate. Very new science suggests that it may be closely related to receptor networks for oxytocin, a neurotransmitter implicated in trust and maternal bonding.

When someone says "…I trust my instinct", they could also say "…I trust my vagus nerve" since instincts are emotional intuitions transferred to the brain through the vagus nerve. As in any mind-body feedback loop, the messages also travel in the opposite direction, that is, from the conscious mind through the vagus nerve to the organs, either to indicate that we are in a moment of calm or in a dangerous situation. to prepare the body for a "fight or flight".

Our autonomic nervous system is made up of two opposing systems that create a tug-of-war in our minds.

The sympathetic nervous system is geared towards putting your foot down on the gas as it feeds on adrenaline and cortisol and is part of the fight or flight response.

The parasympathetic nervous system is the polar opposite. The vagus nerve is the central axis of the functioning of the parasympathetic nervous system. This is geared towards slowing down and uses neurotransmitters like acetylcholine to slow down your heart rate, blood pressure, and help your heart and organs slow down.

Selective stimulation of the vagus nerve is used in some medical treatments, for example, it is regularly used in people suffering from depression, it is also applied in some cases to treat epilepsy.

— Stress and the Vagus Nerve

Your body's stress hormone levels are regulated by the autonomic nervous system (ANS). The ANS has two components that balance each other, the sympathetic nervous system (SNS) and the parasympathetic nervous system (PNS). The SNS increases the activity of the nervous system. It helps us manage what we perceive to be emergencies and is in charge of the flight-fight response. The PNS decreases the activity of the nervous system and helps us stay calm. It promotes relaxation, rest, sleep, and drowsiness by slowing our heart rate, which slows our breathing, constricts the pupils of the eyes, increases saliva production in the mouth, and so on. Acetylcholine is responsible for learning and memory. It is also calming and relaxing, it is used by the vagus nerve to send messages of peace and relaxation throughout the body. New research has found that acetylcholine acts as a major brake on inflammation in the body. In other words, by stimulating the vagus nerve you send acetylcholine throughout your body, not only relaxing you, but also quenching the fire of inflammation that is associated with the negative effects of stress.

The motion behind the Tangasm

Tango is a feeling that can be a cocktail of six basic emotions: happiness, sadness, anger, disgust, surprise and fear. But it is the movement that gives the body to the tango dance that consists of six Pilates principles: breathing, concentration, center, control, precision and flow. The way in which each person integrates these principles in the dance of tango and in life itself is individual. For example, a person may emphasize physical aspects more, improve sports performance, improve muscle tone. Another person may give more importance to the mental aspects, to reduce stress or help improve focus and concentration in their life. However, the important thing is that the execution of each exercise and the practice of the system as a whole.

— Breath

Although all the foundation principles share equal importance, the importance of breath and its numerous implications can be observed far beyond the fundamental and crucial role of respiration. In this view breath can serve as a common thread that runs through all the foundation principles, in a sense sewing them together. Breath is one of the keys to life itself—the respiratory muscles are the only skeletal muscles essential to life—and yet breath is so often taken for granted. An understanding of the anatomy underlying breath can facilitate optimal use of breath. Because of the complex anatomical processes involved in breathing.

— Concentration

Concentration can be defined as direction of attention to a single objective, in this case the mastery of a given dance exercise. A tango practitioner's intent is to perform the exercises as correctly as his or her current skill level will allow. This requires concentration. Begin by going through a mental checklist of points to focus on for each exercise. This may take a few seconds or even a minute or two and should include awareness of the breath pattern as well as the muscles that are about to be worked. Concentrate on the alignment of the body and on maintaining correct alignment and stabilization throughout the execution of the exercise. Maintain mental concentration for the duration of the session.

— Center

The concept of center can have several levels of meaning. Primarily it relates to the body's center of gravity. The body's center of gravity is the single point about which every particle of its mass is equally distributed—the point at which the body could be suspended and where it would be totally balanced in all directions.

Each person is built differently and has an individual center of gravity. Where the center of gravity lies distinctly affects how an exercise feels and how difficult or easy it is to execute. Therefore, it is a mistake to assume a person lacks strength if he cannot execute an exercise successfully. Lack of success may have more to do with how the person is built and the distribution of body weight. When standing upright with the arms down by the sides, the center of gravity of the average person is located just in front of the second sacral vertebra and at about 55 percent of the person's height. However, significant variances can be observed within, as well as between, genders.

Center also relates to the core and the muscles of the core. Center also may have a more esoteric connotation, referring to a feeling of balance within or the eternal spring of energy from which all movement emanates.

— Control

Control can be defined as the regulation of the execution of a given action. Refining control is inherent in mastering a skill.

The first time someone executes an exercise, he or she has to use control, but as skill increases, this control will be more refined.

You can see a distinct difference when viewing a movement performed by someone who has achieved a high level of control and someone who has not.

Often a higher level of control is associated with fewer and smaller errors, exact alignment, greater coordination, greater balance, and greater ability to reproduce the exercise successfully over multiple attempts, using less effort and avoiding excessive muscle tension.

Refined control requires a great deal of practice, which can aid in developing the necessary strength and flexibility of key muscles as well as allow for the development of more refined motor programs.

This practice can also allow these motor programs to run with less conscious attention, so that attention can be paid to finer details and to making minute adjustments, only when needed.

— Precision

Precision can be described as the exact manner in which an action is executed.

Often the exercise itself is not so different from other exercise regimens, but the way it is executed is different.

Knowledge of anatomy aids greatly in achieving precision.

You will understand which muscles are working or should be working.

You will align your body correctly and understand the goals of an exercise.

The greater the precision, the more likely the goal will be achieved and the greater the benefit from doing the exercise.

Precision can be associated with the activation of isolated muscles and at the same time with the integration of the required muscles to create movement.

Precision can make the difference between accessing a muscle or not and between achieving the goal or not.

— Flow

Flow is an essential quality to strive for. Flow can be described as a smooth, uninterrupted continuity of movement.

Romana Kryzanowska describes the Pilates method as "flowing motion outward from a strong center."

Flow requires a deep understanding of the movement and incorporates precise muscle activation and timing.

As movement proficiency develops from extensive practice, each movement and each session should flow. Some approaches also encourage a more esoteric use of flow. This meaning is exemplified in the statement by Mihály Csíkszentmihályi that "flow is the mental state of operation in which the person is fully immersed in what he or she is doing by a feeling of energized focus, full involvement, and success in the process of the activity."

— A Closer Look at the Science of Breathing

Breath is the first principle mentioned in this chapter and one that, historically, has played a vital role in most mind–body systems. Discussions and, at times, disagreements as to a particular breath pattern, or whether a set breath pattern is necessary at all, may arise. However, few people would dispute the importance of breath for exercise, and a better understanding of breathing can help you obtain greater benefits from the exercises in this book.

The major function of the respiratory system is to deliver oxygen to and remove carbon dioxide from the tissues of the body. Although every cell in the body must have oxygen to live, the body's need to rid itself of carbon dioxide, a by-product of cellular metabolism, is the most important stimulus for breathing in a healthy person. At least four processes are involved, collectively termed respiration. The first two processes, external respiration, involve movement of external air into the lungs (pulmonary ventilation) and from the lungs into the blood (pulmonary diffusion), and vice versa. This book will focus on these first two processes. The next two processes involve the transport of gases by the circulatory system to tissues such as muscles and the exchange of oxygen and carbon dioxide between the capillary blood and tissue cells.

— Anatomy of the Respiratory System

The lungs of an average-size person weigh about 2.2 pounds (1 kg). They are compact and fit within the thoracic cavity. However, because of the extensive network of tubes and millions of gas-filled air spaces (alveoli), if spread out the tissue would occupy a surface area about the size of a singles tennis court or a medium-size swimming pool. This unique structure provides the lungs with a massive surface area that is ideal for their vital function of gas exchange.

Structurally, the respiratory system can be divided into two major parts— the upper and lower respiratory tracts. The upper respiratory tract is a system of interconnecting cavities and tubes (nasal cavity, oral cavity, pharynx, and larynx) that provide a pathway for the air into the lower respiratory tract. This upper tract also serves to purify, warm, and humidify the air before it reaches the final portion of the lower tract. The lower respiratory tract (trachea, bronchi, bronchioles, and alveoli) terminates in structures that allow for the exchange of gases, including approximately 300 million alveoli and their associated extensive network of capillaries. The wall of an alveolus is thinner than a piece of tissue paper, easily allowing for oxygen to pass from the alveolus into the tiny pulmonary capillaries and for carbon dioxide to pass from the pulmonary capillaries into the alveolus by simple diffusion.

— Mechanics of Breathing

Pulmonary ventilation, commonly termed breathing, consists of two phases. The process of moving air into the lungs is called inhalation or inspiration, and the process of moving gases out of the lungs is called exhalation or expiration. In essence, pulmonary ventilation is a mechanical process that involves volume changes in the thoracic cavity that lead to pressure changes, which result in the flow of gases to equalize pressures. The changes in volume necessary for pressure changes are greatly aided by the structure of the thorax (sternum, ribs with associated cartilages, and vertebrae). The ribs articulate with the spine so that they can move upward and outward during inspiration and downward and inward during expiration.

— Inhalation

Inhalation (inspiration) is initiated by activation of the respiratory muscles, particularly the diaphragm. When the dome-shaped diaphragm contracts, it flattens out, allowing more height in the thoracic cavity. The external intercostals act to lift the rib cage and pull the sternum forward. The orientation of the ribs is such that the ribs of the midthorax and lower thorax increase volume more laterally, or sideways, while the ribs of the upper thoracic cavity increase thoracic volume more in a forward and backward direction. The increase in volume of the thoracic cavity produced by these respiratory muscles results in the pressure within the alveoli of the lungs (intrapulmonary pressure) being lower than the outside atmospheric pressure. Thus, air enters the lungs until the intrapulmonary pressure is equal to the atmospheric pressure (the pressure exerted by the air outside the body).

The expansion of the lungs is also aided by an additional mechanism relating to the surface tension between two important membranes. These two thin membranes are called pleurae. The visceral pleura covers the lungs, and the parietal pleura covers the inside of the chest wall and diaphragm. Between these two pleurae, the pleural space exists. It is airtight and contains a small amount of fluid. As the chest wall expands, the lungs are drawn outward, coupling the outer covering of the lungs with the inner lining of the thorax wall because of the increase of the negative pressure in the pleural space.

When pulmonary ventilation demands increase, such as during rigorous exercise or with some pulmonary diseases, the two previously described processes are aided by activation of many other accessory muscles. During inspiration, for example, additional muscles such as the scalenes, sternocleidomastoid, pectoralis major, and pectoralis minor can be recruited to help further elevate the ribs. Muscles such as the erector spinae can help straighten the thoracic curve so that a greater increase in thoracic volume precipitates a greater volume of incoming air.

— Exhalation

Exhalation (expiration) with quiet breathing is primarily passive, relying on the elastic recoil of the lung tissue and changes associated with relaxation of the respiratory muscles. As the diaphragm relaxes, it moves upward into the thorax. The ribs lower as the intercostal muscles relax (figure 1.3). The thoracic cavity volume decreases. This, in turn, increases the intrapulmonary pressure relative to the outside atmospheric pressure, resulting in air flowing from the lungs to outside the body.

However, when exhalation is forced, such as when pulmonary ventilation requirements increase, active contraction of many muscles can be added to the passive mechanisms. For example, contraction of the abdominal muscles can press the diaphragm upward via intra-abdominal pressure as well as aid other muscles such as the internal intercostals, quadratus lumborum, and latissimus dorsi in depressing the rib cage.

— Breathing During the dancing of the tango

The belief that breathing exercises, or voluntarily controlled breathing patterns, may provide health benefits or enhance physical performance has been shared by many cultures for centuries. The proposed benefits range from enhanced relaxation and decreased stress to lowered blood pressure, improved focus, activation of specific muscles, better circulation and respiration, and even lowered risk for cardiovascular disease. Although some scientific research exists regarding the potential positive effects of various controlled breathing techniques, additional research is needed to better understand these benefits and create optimal training techniques. However, one cannot ignore the number of disciplines, both Eastern and Western, that use breath in a profound way—yoga, tai chi, aikido, karate, capoeira, dance, swimming, weightlifting, and so on. Some systems of training have endeavored to harness different effects of breath to enhance performance or foster health of the body, mind, and spirit.

— Daily energy routine exercise for dancing the Tango

In Chapter 3 The Tango Lesson we have recommended Donna Eden's exercises as in this video:
https://youtu.be/akIlrF-HSJM
The best music to practice these exercises is the music "Queen Bee - Ajai Alai" which contains the musical structure of a tango (question, pause, answer) and a wide variety of instruments to move the body according to the rhythm or melody:
https://youtu.be/M2t1F0EIgUg

The teaching to achieve a Tangasm

Ricardo Vidort (1929 – 2006) is considered as "the last Milonguero" of Buenos Aires, and perhaps also the "supreme teacher" of teaching the tango for social purposes. Following are Ricardo's notes on his tango classes:

"Most of you beginners decide to learn tango because you have seen tango shows, stage dancers or championships, and you really think that this is the real tango. Here is where you are mistaken.

Why? Because this kind of tango is for a show, a stage; it's not the real tango, the one that thousands danced on the streets and milongas of Buenos Aires.

The traditional tango style is feeling!

Get the rhythm and put it into everything–your dreams, thoughts, love, passion, because when you put it all together, that's feeling!

Begin to walk with this beat of tango, and you will have your own style!

— The essence of a Tango Class:

Once you understand and know how to walk with rhythm, you will begin to dance in a couple.

When you go to the dance floor:

Women should stand with their backs to the tables, because her first step will be to her right.

Men, on the contrary, should stand with their backs to the center of the dance floor, because their first step is with the left foot.

Both have to walk or dance, in that way, counter-clockwise around the room.

This is the correct way to dance–keeping a distance from the couple ahead and the one behind you. We call this "handling the floor."

Remember that you dance for your own pleasure and joy, and not for the people. No one can invent a new step, no one is the owner of steps, but yes, you are the owner of your style because this is only made by your feeling.

Relax and breathe
Hear and listen to the music…
Elegance in your walking and posture
Now regulate your steps with the concept of the rhythm (beat)
Ladies: wait for the man
You are dancing the tango!!!
Note: No teacher, academy or school can teach feeling. That's yours and from it comes your own style.

— Teaching the Tango in eight classes

First class: Explain how to relax; Walk to get the rhythm; Begin with the correct position
Second class: How to embrace and walk together
Third class: Walking backwards and forwards together and crossing
Fourth class: How to turn to the right
Fifth class: How to turn to the left
Sixth class: Corridas forward
Seventh class: Corridas backward
Eighth class: Let's begin to dance the tango!

— The fundamentals of a tango class

1) Embrace, feeling
2) Develop your feeling, give it to your partner
3) Body has a muscular receiver
4) Feet and chest — at the same time.
5) Energy – how it influences the third Chakra (solar plexus) in both.
6) Elegance comes when you walk with the music in a natural way.
7) Dance for your partner, not for others (social tango).
8) The woman and the music are always first.

— The notes of a tango class

1) Tango Milonguero style, what is it?
2) Steps and feeling
3) Dancing tango in different expressions of the feeling (with the same steps) i.e. — D'Arienzo and Fresedo
4) Does the body think, where is dancing?
5) Why 7 steps make all the tango. How many combinations are there?
6) What is first, the music or the steps and figures?
7) Elegance is walking, what the man does to distribute his strength and energy to the woman, and vice versa
8) Evolution and involution of tango as a dance.

— The demonstrations of a tango class

1) Postures — feminine and masculine: embrace, axis, the body angle
2) Position, importance of the chakras
3) How the man leads, how the woman receives the lead (waiting)
4) The importance of the footwork, the metatarsal – its force and direction

5) Walking in its three forms: left, right, and center
6) Rotations to change the direction; Turns to the left and right
7) "Corridas" (fast walk): forward, side, backward, and circular
8) Puentes, calecitas, balanceo, hamacando (sway), cadencia, pauses

—   The rhythms of a tango class

1) Syncopation, rhythm
2) Improvisation
3) Perceptions
4) Compatibility
5) "Engaños" (misleads)
6) "Arranques" (starting motion)
7) Time and space
8) Understanding of music: question, pause, answer

—   The concepts of a tango class

1) Relaxation
2) Sensibility
3) Confidence
4) Peacefulness
5) Change of weight with each step
6) Magnetism of the music in the body
7) Energy
8) Breathing

—   Is the real essence of tango dying? Why? (Academies are all the same)

The first phase of tango is in its history, how it originated, different influences of other music, rhythms, and especially how the musicians and musicians felt it. History of different orchestras (Canaro, Di Sarli, Biaggi, etc).

The entire aspect of tango has a physical and spiritual force. A teacher should see in each student his or her own feeling, which is different from everybody else, and within it correct and emanate the suitable.

Relaxation… it brings sensitivity, confidence, stillness, weight change with each step and the magnetism of music on the body.

Don't start by teaching steps and figures, for God's sake!"

https://ricardovidort.wordpress.com/teaching/

III. The secrets of the Tango Milonguero in Buenos Aires

"The tango is a feeling. It is not difficult to learn. Nor is it easy. But it is not danced by figures and steps. It is danced to the music. Dance the music. Because the music is the tango." ~ Pedro Alberto Rusconi (1936 - 2010) https://youtu.be/YFdcMvRL3no

The Tango Milonguero is the Tango of the Golden Age between 1936 and 1955, the tango "cortado" (half cut). It is the tango created by the middle class of the Nationalist era, also known as National Tango, danced in Milongas and Confectioneries. In truth, Tango Milonguero is a hybrid tango between the Aristocratic Tango "sin corte" (without cut) of the New Guard (1914 – 1936) and the Tango Criollo "con corte" (with cut) of the Old Guard (1890 – 1914).

Once a young fellow told to an old Milonguero « I took several tango classes, and they tell me that there is no other way to "mark" than with the torso! Is it true? because there are fashions that are imposed as absolute statements and I remember other approaches such as "mark with everything we have at hand". »
Let me answer to this question by using a couple of examples.

— The embrace

Graciela Gonzalez, a great teacher whom I respect, always says that you have to embrace in tango like you would hug a friend you love, someone you appreciate, that is, with both arms around her torso, with love. If we start dancing like this, then we will open the hug naturally, just enough to be able to mark and move, while letting go of the left hand and taking the woman's right hand with it.

— The surrender

Something fundamental that is often forgotten is that if there is no surrender from the woman, there is no true embrace. That surrender does not consist only of squeezing, it is tenderness, softness, relaxation, trust and letting the man do what he can lead her and mark her without problems. It is basic, deliver the torso, the chest, opening the shoulders while they relax. In this position, well in front of the man, not half to the side, and holding firmly to the ground, one begins to dance, or rather, to walk. A few small steps and a silence to stand up and resume the posture, relax the shoulders and keep them facing each other. If there is no surrender (from the man too), little can be done.

— The mark

It is marked "with everything", as Carlos Gavito said, "even with the hairs of the mustache".

« The woman should not think, she should not break her head trying to guess what her partner is telling her.

If she doesn't get a clear mark, she shouldn't do anything.

There are no predetermined movements in tango, small choreographies or obvious steps that women have to do automatically.

You also mark with your eyes.

You have to stop, pause, concentrate and look your partner in the eye, gently, perhaps out of the corner of your eye, thinking about what you want to mark.

That's when the intention is gently advanced, » he said.

— The intent

But, how to transmit what we want to mark?

You have to gently advance the mark, without dissociating the arms from the torso, with which the mark is slightly started.

At that time, you have to hold her gently to try to keep her from moving beyond what is desired.

She moves just enough to transmit this message to the man:

« I understood you », and she waits for him in the same position, without changing weights.

To advance the mark, perhaps a slight gesture is enough, just like her to answer him.

From there, she can already walk in unison.

The intention is transmitted more with the brain than with the body itself, which is more real than it seems.

— The hold

We must, for comfort, not "wring" our partner's hands.

Once with the palm of the hand extended, we take hers and we can close it a little and turn it too, without exaggeration.

There is a tension that allows the mark to be transmitted, but there is no force, because it is marked with the torso.

The hands are the ends of the arms, which accompany the torso in its movements, in any case they are a limit for them.

Height: I would say that the shoulders or slightly above them, if the woman is somewhat less tall or equal to the man.

— The energy

How can we mark our partner without suffocating her in a hug that is too close, without pushing her, and without moving her with her arms so as not to unbalance her?

Imagine that the man forms with his torso and arms a "U", or almost a circle, in which there is a magnetic field and inside, his partner, who must be made to move with that energy and only use physical contact of the torso to transfer the intention, both when starting to dance and in all subsequent movements. You have to do it gently, with hardly any force.

The arms, just to contain her, to keep her within the "magnetic" field.

If the torsos are not well faced and very close, the energy cannot be transmitted. And if these are facing each other, the rest of the trunk, including the shoulders, should also be facing each other, for the same reason.

The head always in the axis of the trunk, never putting weight on that of our partner. If we get tense and stiff, which is very common, it happens like a short-circuit. It takes a certain flexibility and relaxation (in both) to transmit the message gently, with love, with feeling.

We must be well established on the floor, without bending or bending and from that firm step (with the whole foot), transfer the energy "of the whole body", to our partner. By doing it this way, that hug will be both comfortable and elegant; we will have found "our" embrace, that point of balance that is different for each one.

— The stepping

According to the milonga master Raúl Cabral, the body must move (that is, change weight) with the leg that supports the weight of the body itself and not with the leg that is free of weight. The weight-bearing leg gives the push, pushes, and then makes the whole body do the movement.

Try to shift your weight – making a step forward - with your free leg and stop (1). Then I suggest you do another switch, but this time with the weight-bearing leg (2). You will notice that if you do the weight shift (1) with the free leg, you will first put the foot on the ground and then the body weight will come (wrong movement).

If, on the other hand, the body moves with the leg that supports its weight (2), all the weight of the body arrives together at the same time, at the support of the foot with the free leg on the ground (correct movement).

You have to feel the difference! It is very, very big.

In the right way, second option, your body acquires presence, soul, volume, and from now on it will be a body that speaks, that transmits, a tango body.

— The tempo

The widespread 2x4 rhythm with which tango is usually identified no longer exists and fell early - even before the 1940s - into total disuse. Only the first tangos were set to music in 2x4 time (two white notes per measure).

The tempo of tango is four by eight (four beats, in eighth notes in each measure). For this reason, tango has traditionally been danced with four steps, joining in the fourth, except if the bullfight is performed. This allows you to step on all four beats, one step per beat. To dance tango, all you need to do is walk with this basic core of four steps, to the beat. Dancing is moving, moving to the beat of music and, if that music is tango, tango is being danced. Figures can then be added. But the fundamental thing is to "walk the tango" and that means within the tempo.

When the dancer is done, he seeks to find the first beat of each measure with his first step (left foot), thus not only marking the beats, but also performing each core of the four basic steps within the measure. For this, he marks that first step more strongly and almost automatically he will find the strong beat of each measure, which is the first. And so, when he finishes the tango, he will finish it right with the last footsteps (closing).

The fundamental deformation of current dance tango is that it is danced, in the vast majority of cases, without considering the beat. Because a way of dancing has emerged that does not allow the beat to be taken. You go out - and teach yourself to go out - with the right foot (the man) backwards and take five steps, joining in the fifth. Then it continues with three steps, joining in the third. As can be seen, it does not allow dancing to the tempo of the style with a five-beat back start. This output can be used on some occasion as a figure, knowing that there will be a problem with the tempo, to be solved. But never as a basic nucleus that is repeated permanently, as is done with the four steps.

The problem is even more difficult when dancing a tango by the Old Guard or simply a Juan D'Arienzo, for example, where the first chord usually lasts a beat and a half, the second half a beat and the remaining two one each. In this case, the dancer, if he wants to dance to the beat, has to make a long and slow step (one and a half), a short step (half a beat) to continue with a beat and a beat. This is the "corrida" (fast walk or run). Also, four steps but with different values and marked by the musicians.

The discomfort of dancing out of time makes the dancers take refuge in the figures, to try to hide the lack of harmony between music and dance. By permanently performing figures without "walking" the tango, the rhythm disappears, and a hybrid dance is seen, which is performed with tango music in the background, but which could be the Marseillaise.

In traditional tango, after each figure you must "walk" to recover the tempo, which in the figure could have been diluted a bit.

In the fifties, those who did pure turns were called "calesiteros" and those who only made figures, without cutting them with walks, "verduleros".

While the tango is being danced, the dancers are immersed in the music and perform as if they were part of the orchestra. In those moments there are no other interests than dancing harmoniously, delivered to each other. In tango, sensuality must be present in the movements, not sexuality. It must be a totally spontaneous dance, of permanent creativity. If you want to dance tango properly, you must arrive on the dance floor without knowing what you are going to do. And there are not a few times that new steps arise during the dance. If one remembers them, incorporates them and has them in the arsenal.

Tango, when tied to a predetermined choreography, is a mechanical dance, where the dancers are tied to certain steps without being able to express what they feel at that moment. It is not the same as a dancer dancing with one woman or another, even if both are excellent dancers. The fundamental thing is the communication that is established between the two. If there is, there will be a beautiful tango dancing, even if they have only walked it.

It must be regretted that the gap left by a generation without tango has deteriorated the transmission of the memory of the tango dance.

— The cadence

The cadence in the dance could be defined as the way of interpreting the music. It is the measure of the sound, of the music, that each dancer interprets in a certain way with her bodily expression. But always within the rhythmic guidelines that marks the score. For a certain rhythm, different cadences fit. Associate the cadence to the pause, to the way of express the dancing of adagios, the beginnings and ends of a verse, of a musical phrase.

Having said all this, some concepts become clearer:

1. That the cadence, more or less, is the way of interpreting the music, said in a generic way. Cadence is something that, unlike technique, does not admit exact or precise definitions, but that marks and determines the seal, the personal style of a dancer.

2. That it has to do with the measure, with the accentuation, with the pauses (in prose and verse). These concepts are the ones that also define a certain cadence in the dance. They serve to interpret music in one way or another. Each one of us interprets it in a different and personal way, because we hear it differently, because it suggests different sensations to us. Perhaps sadness, tenderness, in a passage that we dance lightly, but that makes others happy, and they dance it with more energy. Someone in that same musical passage, can let their imagination fly for a moment and pause, because they feel that need, because they have to enjoy that moment.

3. That is expressed with the whole body: "The dancer expresses his art with the body. The aesthetics of dance is body expression." The only cadence, an adequate musical interpretation is not enough to classify, to assess a way of dancing (as good, bad, correct or incorrect). Because the most important thing would be missing, the artistic expression. That itself cannot be defined, I think, or classified. Dancing tango, there are those who for years of doing it, incorporated a cadence, a form of musical expression in their correct dance, we would say, even good. But from that to being able to say, "dancing well", my friends, there is a long way to go. You can be handsome or ugly, have a good appearance or not, which helps of course, but art... they have very few. And to dance well you have to have art.

What is art, huh?

"What does not leave others indifferent, what makes you feel when you see it, even transforms you."

"It is the result of creativity, of the ability to transmit emotion, sensations."

"It is the ability to improvise and react to a stimulus, music, in this case, without always doing the same thing, creating".

— Final notes

It is clear that it is marked with the whole body, with the whole body as a unit. But the main message is emitted from the torso. Because the partner cannot be attentive to all parts of the body.

From the torso the intention of the movement is advanced in a first moment.

When we "hook", that is, in that second instant that we verify that she understood the direction and direction of the step, we mark the length of it and go with her.

In the next step, the musical cadence will be marked. The arms do not move independently of the torso, their role is to help transmit the mark at the same time as the torso and gently contain the dancer within them.

That role is fundamental in her walk, where they help her to go at the same time as her dancer, containing her, gently stopping her when she advances and making her pass through her axis at the same time as the one who leads her.

If we notice that she is going to go beyond her, we will hold her firmly if necessary, before she moves beyond her axis, then we will make her wait.

We will do it with her right arm (hand and forearm) and raising her a little to prevent her from stepping on it.

So, we step both at the same time. If despite everything she continues, if she gets ahead, we have no choice but to go with her, we must not stay behind.

To pass through her axis and avoid getting ahead, she must bring her feet together, pass with which she moves next to the other, in each movement.

There she will make a very slight stop on the road, taking advantage of it to gently support with the leg that moves from her.

There, on the axis, she will always wait for the man to keep up with him.

The leg that comes, does not go through the air, nor just separated from the other.

This is true for both walks and turns.

The same goes for turns.

On right turns, the left arm. ours is "welded" to the torso and goes with it. Both, torso and left arm, advance the mark, transfer the intention. And the right arm contains her body, it's as if when she goes, she says « eye, up to here. »

In left turns, the role of the arms is reversed.

If there are doubts, be clear: the mark, the intention, begins in the torso, in its center and the arms go with it.

The worst thing a dancer can do is punch with their arms or initiate a step with their feet, a kick out with their legs, or a twist with their hips.

Here a list of interviews with the old Milongueros of Buenos Aires:
https://youtube.com/playlist?list=PLdqlIO6icahHTVlp5i_zvEP7jWOTOiNfI

"I think those who say that you can't tango if you are not Argentinian are mistaken. Tango was an immigrant music... so it does not have a nationality. It is only passport is feeling." ~ Carlos Gavito (1942-2005)

IV. The secrets of the Tango de Salon in Buenos Aires

« Without "firuletes" (choreographic embellishments), tango has to be walked. When he taught me dancing he used to tell me: "You have to take long strides. And a man has to know how to hold a woman". That was an elegant, refined, aristocratic dancing. » ~ Vicente Madero's daughter Malú Madero de Fernández Ocampo explaining his father way of dancing the tango.
https://www.todotango.com/english/artists/biography/1605/Vicente-Madero/

The Tango de Salon is the Tango of the New Guard between 1914 and 1936 (the tango without court). It is the tango created by the upper class of the Art Deco era danced in Salons and Cabarets also known as Aristocratic Tango.

The Argentinian author Victoria Ocampo has recalled in her testimonies:

« The time came when every Thursday, rain or shine, Osvaldo Fresedo, El Pibe de La Paternal, entered the house and tango was danced the entire afternoon. The champions of these memorable days were Ricardo Güiraldes (author of the novel Don Segundo Sombra), with no more celebrity than what we, his friends, suspected he would achieve, and Vicente Madero, a genius on the matter and I don't think anyone have gotten over it. When he walked the tango, his whole body, apparently immobile, elastically followed the rhythm, lived it, communicated it to his companion who, infected, obeyed that perfect and measured walk. They were both perfect dancers."

When did these tango parties take place?

Undoubtedly, after 1913, the year in which the Sociedad Sportiva — presided over by Antonio De Marchi — organized the famous Palace Theater competition, of which Madero was a member of the jury, together with Daniel Videla Dorna and the musician Antonio Chimenti, and which was presided over by another musician, the pianist and composer Julián Aguirre, founder of the Escuela Argentina de Música. And before 1920, when Madero was a regular in Parisian cabarets, including the Princesse, where he took Manuel Pizarro to play bandoneon and whose owner, Elio Volterra, was convinced by him to change his name and it was renamed "El Garrón".

The Tango de Salón was developed to dance in the aristocracy ballrooms of the Barrio Norte in Buenos Aires, at their parties in Mar del Plata, at the carnivals of the Teatro Colón in the city of Rosario, or in the famous Parisian-inspired cabarets such as Armenonville, Chantecler, Tabarís, etc, accompanied by the orchestras of Francisco Canaro, Roberto Firpo, Eduardo Arolas, Juan Maglio, Juan D'Arienzo, Osvaldo Fresedo, etc.

The best-known dance teachers of the Tango de Salon for the high society of Buenos Aires were Nicanor Lima, Manuel E. Silva, Domingo Gaeta and Count Juan E. de Chikoff, the inventor of the tango step "1— 2, 3, 4 close and cross".

All have focused on teaching dance with elegance, aesthetics and good manners, but it has been Count Juan E. Chikoff who has written an article about the secret of dancing Tango de Salon, for both sexes, in Florida magazine No. 2, dated July 21, 1925:

"YOU HAVE TO LEARN TO DANCE!

In my previous lesson, as the readers will remember, I have directed almost all of my indications towards the gentlemen, considering that the teaching of the dance, for the men, is much more difficult and more important than for the feminine sex; but before getting into the matter, I will make a few small observations and indications, for the ladies and gentlemen.

The mission of the female sex in the dance is less important than that of the gentlemen and consists solely of following and interpreting the dancer's instructions in time.

Most of the ladies and girls, because of the slenderness and natural grace of their bodies, are good dancers.

It is noticeable that there is an enormously great defect in a large number of them: they become very heavy, although their natural weight is that of feathers.

The heaviness of the dancers comes from misinterpreting good posture when dancing.

Generally, the representatives of the fair sex, with their fine and delicious right arm, support the total weight of their body on the gentleman's left, tiring him so much that the dance is transformed instead of pleasure into torment, and as no dancer dares to tell a lady or girl that she is heavy, she resigns herself during the execution of the entire dance piece.

It is the greatest defect of the ladies, in which they incur against their will and without realizing it; but that defect is simply corrected.

The ladies and gentlemen must concentrate the weight of their entire body on the waist, and instead of pressing with the right arm from the top downwards, which is defective, they must do it from the bottom upwards and hold the right arm by their own strength. and not lean on the partner's left arm.

The gentleman should feel on his left arm a gentle touch of the companion's right arm and not his weight, just as the companion's left arm must rest gently on the gentleman's right shoulder with the tips of the fingers, always supported by your own effort.

The correct and elegant posture of the body of the dancers is almost equal to that of the gentleman.

The partner's head should look to the left side, the body straight, naturally, shoulders slumped, knees the same as those of the gentleman, neither bent nor hard, but flexible and the feet on half point, in tango and in the other dances: reminding them that the gentlemen must dance the tango on the entire sole of the foot and the ladies on the midpoint.

You also have to be very careful not to jump in the dance, and not to raise your feet more than necessary, which some dancers do especially in tango, believing that they are doing the dance with more mastery.

Do not forget that no one sees himself dancing.

The dancers must never indicate to the dancer, either with the movement of the body or the arms, any step or figure while dancing, but rather give themselves completely to the dance of the gentleman and try in the best way to follow it.

Otherwise, it turns out that the gentleman who has the initiative in the dance tries to make some figure, the partner hinders him, wanting to make another figure, then that is when the annoying stomping begins, and complete demoralization takes over the spirit of the dancer who he loses the serenity and the skill of the dance, especially if the dancer is a beginner, due to which the exclamations of: « I can't dance with him », or « I can't dance with her », things that should never happen, because the dancer, if he dances more than his partner, has to adapt to her dance and not make difficult figures that won't be able to be executed by the partner, and vice versa, the dancer should not trust too much in the dancer that she sees that he does not dance very well and try to interpret the instructions of the partner, even if they are bad.

In this way the dance will always be harmonious.

In general, the dance of the ladies and girls depends only on the good direction of the gentlemen: so right now, I will try in the best possible way to explain the way of conducting to the companion.

In my previous lesson I said that the teaching of dance in general and of tango in particular, is divided into three parts and that they are the following: elegance, theory and the way of carrying it.

What we lack is the third and that is knowing how to make the companion understand the steps and figures that one is going to do.

The most important and main role here is played by the right arm, on which the entire dance depends, which is as if it were the rudder of a ship, if I may be so compared.

The right arm is placed a little above the waist, more or less in the middle of the partner's back, the fingers stretched and well joined, supported with the entire palm of the hand, and it is essential throughout the dance to have a muscular tension of the arm and forearm, and gently pressing the partner's back with the hand. So before doing any step, with the right hand we indicate to the partner the movement, what we are going to do, because the mission of ladies in the dance - as I have already said - is to follow every dancer, good or bad, knowing how to smoothly and agilely fill instantly with his foot the void produced by the dancer's foot.

For example: we intend to go back with the left foot, so we make a little pressure with the right hand on the right side of the partner's back, thus forcing her to go out with the right foot.

We want to make the figure from the side, so with the forearm we put pressure on the left side of the partner, indicating with this our intention to leave the side.

If we want to make a turn, either advancing or retreating, and knowing the foot with which we advance or retreat, we put pressure on the right or left side of the partner's back, forcing her to come out with the foot we want and in the moment of turning around, we gently press the arm, forearm and hand on the waist of the partner, indicating our intentions with this, and in the same way we proceed to make any other figure.

So, always the right arm must feel the partner and gently press in such a way that she could not make any other movement that is not the will of the dancer.

But it never means that with that I give my opinion that it is necessary to squeeze the partner to be able to dance well.

Never, because only a gentle pressure on the back is enough for the partner to understand what step one is going to take.

Warning them that in the way of carrying the ladies and girls, the cradle, education and culture of the gentleman is revealed.

Modern dance is a complement to education, it is a hobby, it is a more pleasant exercise, it is a finishing touch with which all social gatherings are closed, and it is necessary to seek only sociability, elegance, grace in dance. and aesthetics.

I will explain the music of modern dances in general and of tango in particular and the application of steps towards it.

Formerly, the presence of the dance master was required in the great festas, so that he could guide the audience on steps and figures that had to be executed during the dance.

At that time the dance had been arranged for the music and during the execution of the dances as Cuadrillas, Roman-Dance, Lancers or some other dance piece, to the voice of the teacher, steps were executed, whether waltz, polka, mazurka or some other figures and the spectator saw that all the dancers made identical movements.

Currently that does not happen.

The dance is not arranged for the music, such and such figures are not required for this or that rhythm, rather, the music is arranged for the dance.

The beat of a tango or a fox-trot is uniform from the beginning to the end.

The only thing that varies is the melody, to which you can start dancing and do any step exactly, even once the music has started halfway, or when it comes to an end, and that is why everyone dances differently, and they make the figures that they like the most.

The beat of the tango is extremely simple, and I repeat, as I said in my first lesson, that a special ear is not necessary, but it is more difficult to dance outside the beat of the tango, than following it.

The tango beat has four tempos, so any figure that has four foot movements corresponds to a beat.

It is necessary to prolong the first beat and speed up the remaining three in the following way: 1— 2, 3, 4, 1— 2, 3, 4.

For example: we do figure number two, which is backwards, in four movements, stepping back with the left foot, we make a small pause of half a second, and continue the other three movements until we join the feet.

This small pause that we have made after the first half is called the "asentada" ("the sit" or "el corte") , a word that has caused so much horror in the social circles of Paris, where it has been introduced by translating it as "S'assoir", which in Castilian means "to sit", and the French, when doing this "sitting", bent their knees enormously, linking their feet with those of their partner, in an unsightly posture, remaining in it for several seconds and thus killing our much-loved dance.

The "sit" or "el corte" is done only going backwards.

The gentlemen go back with the left foot, slightly bending the left knee and having the right foot completely stretched, supporting the soles of the feet and remaining in this position for barely half a second, and the ladies, when seated, have their right foot advanced completely stretched and on the sole of the foot, leaving the left foot a little behind, brushing the floor with the toe of the shoe.

With this, I have finished explaining the most important indications of tango, and now I will explain to the gentlemen one more figure of tango, which is called the bullfight.

Like all figures, the run is made in four foot movements, and since it is forward, it starts with the right foot.

We stand in a room with our backs to the wall, we advance with the right foot and count one, we continue to advance with the left foot and count two, on the third we unite the right foot with the left, and on the fourth we leave with the left foot, and the run is done.

We will rehearse it several times until we do it without thinking.

The tempo of the bullfight music is always 1— 2, 3, 4.

Once the run is done, we stay with the left foot forward and the right foot behind.

Having the right foot behind, we can make any figure that corresponds to this foot.

With this figure and the other five figures explained in my previous lesson, I conclude the elementary teaching of the theory of tango.

People who did not know how to dance and who have made the effort to practice all the figures explained and all the other indications, by now should already know how to execute them perfectly, and in this way they already have the way open to dance tango.

Interested gentlemen who have ladies or girls in their homes who are also interested in dancing should invite them to serve as dance partners, and in leisure time, to the sound of tango music played by a jukebox, play immediately put into practice all the instructions in the following way: the gentleman will adopt the posture for the dance indicated in my first lesson and taking into account the instructions given in the course of the present one on the way of driving, he will execute the learned figures, trying to do them to the beat of the music in the way already explained.

At first it will be a bit difficult, but we must not forget that perseverance and perseverance overcome all obstacles that arise.

In a brief summary I will remind you that in my two lessons I had explained to you how tango should be danced, the music, the posture of the body, the way of driving and its main steps.

My work is done.

Now it is up to my readers to apply it.

All the other figures of the tango are fantasies and derive from the indicated steps.

Each one must dance the tango as he feels as he interprets the music, always based on his principles. Everyone learned the alphabet in the same way and no two people write a letter the same; the same happens with tango: no two people dance it in the same way.

With this I end my second lesson, and the next one I will dedicate exclusively to American dances, explaining their theory, music and application.

SECOND LESSON OF TANGO by dance teacher JUAN E. DE CHIKOFF"
https://digital.iai.spk-berlin.de/viewer/image/1771993995/55/LOG_0046/
https://digital.iai.spk-berlin.de/viewer/image/1771993995/55/LOG_0047/
https://digital.iai.spk-berlin.de/viewer/image/1771993995/55/LOG_0048/

Here a footage collection from many movies and instructions around the world about the first and initial figure of the tango, known by several names as "la asentada", "la sentada", "el corte", "corte hamacado", "the cortez", "le corté", "le coupé" or "the sit":
https://youtu.be/Z3kNpR1oyBk

The Argentinian style of Tango de Salon is shown in a rare footage in the movie "La Borrachera del Tango" (The Tango Drunkenness") filmed in 1928 based in a theatrical play from 1921 with the same name. It became also a known tango recorded in 1928 by the singer Carlos Gardel and by the Orchestras of Osvaldo Fresedo and Francisco Canaro:
https://youtu.be/TYpRvxxZbJ4

V. The secrets of the Tango Criollo in Buenos Aires

"And tango comes out, not from the people, not from the aristocracy, but from the mixed environment, I believe, from certain "unholy" houses, and I believe that this can be proven by the instruments. If tango had emerged from the people, its instrument would have been the guitar... instead we know that the first tango instruments were the piano, the flute and the violin, to which the bandoneon would later be added. And none of this has to do with the people. All this already presupposes that environment in which the ruffian and the good boy rubbed shoulders, skull.

And I remember those first tangos without lyrics or with obscene lyrics, and I also remember having seen them dance (on the corner of Serrano and Guatemala), having seen tango dance to the beat of the little organ by pairs of men, of men because the women did not want to participate in a dance whose origin they knew.

And I remember that sentence coined by Lugones: "Tango, that reptile of the lupanar". I want to admire the precision of the word "reptile" in which the "cortes y quebradas" (sits and dips) are, the sinuousness of the dance" ~ Jorge Luis Borges (1899 – 1986)

https://www.yumpu.com/en/document/read/14031812/traditional-tango-hector-arico/1

The Tango Criollo is the Tango of the Old Guard between 1890 and 1914 (the tango with "corte"). It is the tango created by the lower class of the Belle Époque era danced in Bailongos (Courtyard street balls) and Dance Houses of not so good reputation.

Angel Villoldo's El Porteñito, is one of the best-known tangos. Composed in 1903, it was among the first to be recorded.

Villoldo called the piece a tango criollo but since the latter half of the 1930s, it has also been performed as a milonga.

Practically all Argentinian movies of the 1930-40s, set in Buenos Aires around the turn of the 20th century, included a dancing scene in which El Porteñito was performed, often at neck-breaking speed.

If it is possible to name one tango that represents Buenos Aires more than any other, it is surely El Porteñito.

The formal structure of El Porteñito is simple and quite symmetric. It consists of three sections of 16 measures each (hereafter identified as A, B, and C).

The three sections are "through-composed" in the score, that is, they are written successively without break and no repetitions are indicated.

Nevertheless, each section ends on a strong cadence that provides a point of incision in the flow of the music and thus sets off one section from the next.

Each section is, in turn, divided into two phrases, antecedent and consequent, of 8 measures (henceforth A1, A2, B1, etc.).

Melodically and harmonically, antecedent and consequent are very similar and differ only in their terminations.

Section A is characterized by lively motives of fast note values in descending motion, leading to short figures of the most characteristic rhythm of tango, the síncopa.

The antecedent and consequent phrases of section B are also very similar.

In contrast to section A, however, the rhythmic movement is calmer due to longer note values and an almost complete avoidance of the síncopa.

It must be noted, nevertheless, that in terms of the fundamental structure of the melodies, sections A and B differ little from each other.

The direction of the melodic movement is complementary (descending) and the target notes of the descending motives correspond as well.

A comparison of the melodic outline of Sections A and B demonstrates clearly the similarities between the two sections.

Section C, by contrast, shows a predominantly upward melodic motion, and there are no síncopas to be found.

As the melodic outline shows, the general movement strives upward and thus creates a contrast to sections A and B.

http://elvictrolerocastizo.blogspot.com/2017/10/a-brief-harmony-of-tango-part-ii.html

The Argentinian film "El canto cuenta su historia" (1976) shows a memory of Angel Villoldo with a record of playing and singing El Porteñito: https://youtu.be/etJ5i95xCBU

The lyrics of El Porteñito and the counterpart female version of La Porteñita were published in the book "La China Feria y Poesías Varias" by Félix Hidalgo and other authors (1909):

TANGO "El Porteñito"

I am a son of Buenos Aires
by nickname the porteñito
the most compadrito Creole
who was born on this earth
when a tango on the vihuela
strum some partner
there is no one in the whole world
who dances better than me

There is none equal to me
to fall in love with women,

pure talk opinions
pure edge and nothing more;
when i face him
I describe her full body
securing the pot
with the money they will give

I am terror of flannels
when I get into a dance
because I respect no one
of those in the meeting;
and if someone gets back
and he comes pretending to be handsome
I send it with a snap.
to find who begot him

When money is already scarce
I make a story for my Creole
who is the most sagacious woman
that she stepped on the neighborhood of the south,
and like broth from heaven
she enters nikel to the pocket
and to the beat of the organ
I dance a tango to her health.

* * * * *

TANGO "La Porteñita"

I am a daughter of Buenos Aires
they call me the porteñita
the most comadrita Creole
who was born on this earth
when a tango on the vihuela
strum some partner
there is no one in the whole neighborhood
who dances better than me

There is no equal to me
to dance a Creole tango
why long the whole roll
when i start to dance
and if any dancer

wants to take over the stop
I leave her embarrassed
and she has to spy

I'm tremendous for the cut
when I get into a dance
why I respect no one
of those who know how to dance
and the one who wants to win me
you have to be very smart
that for tango this Creole
they have to respect her

When money is already scarce
I make a story for my Creole
that he is the most sagacious man,
dancer and good singer
and as fallen from the sky
between the nikel to the pocket
I dance a tango of my flower.

https://digital.iai.spk-berlin.de/viewer/image/835980944/27/
https://digital.iai.spk-berlin.de/viewer/image/835980944/28/
https://digital.iai.spk-berlin.de/viewer/image/835980944/29/

In 1913, the first history written about the tango in Buenos Aires was published in the newspaper "Diario Crítica" by José Antonio Saldías (1891-1946) "El Viejo Tanguero":

"Tango its evolution and its history. Who implanted it."
By José Antonio Saldías "El Viejo Tanguero"
Newspaper "Diario Crítica", September 22, 1913
(José Gobello's archive from the Academia Porteña del Lunfardo)

« No one would have thought in those embryonic eras of cosmopolitanism, that through time and by the reflex action of the progressive movement, that exotic dance that people of color would one day devise could resurface with violent impetus, replacing the devilish candombé of legendary Africans.
The tango, whose baptism certificate was recorded in the popular annals of the old "corralero" neighborhood (current Parque de los Patricios neighborhood), has had an unsuspected resurgence.

It is almost certain that, in the voluminous history of national dances, there is no such case as the one that today concerns public attention, not only in his native land, but also abroad, where he has spread his swaggers with passionate characters.

Until a few years ago, nobody took care of him, except to condemn him for his suburban extravagances.

It was considered as a genuine dance of brave people, of those who send a stab of defiance wrapped in each look.

Today the opinion has changed and on the contrary, it is viewed with sympathy, for the brotherhood of old traditions with vidalitas and sentimental styles.

The black condemnation in which he lived for years due to the undeniable social sentence of adverse theories, has been preceded by an act of gentle amnesty and kind exequatur of vindication.

It was spawned in the underworld, had a parasitic life with malevolent impurities and resurrected the palatial court with the heat of new and exuberant desires.

The republicanism of his parents who ignored the beautiful garments of this son born in fateful days and disastrous lusts, never suspected that he could regenerate and rehabilitate himself at the age of majority to climb the sumptuous precincts of ancient palaces, where the tinsel of noble European lineages.

For this reason, his compatriots today raise a pedestal of honor for him and sing hymns of praise in reparation for the injustice with which he was treated for twenty years.

Now that his name has been imposed in the royal halls of civilized nations, his fellow citizens grant him a letter of honesty for his triumph and welcome him with the trumpets of fame.

So far no one has pointed out the history of this old dance, whose prestige crossed the thresholds of the old world, raising admiration for the most apathetic countries that were always shown by the chords of music foreign to the environment.

Since the social note is concentrated around that dance that little by little has been gaining the will of its own detractors, we want to take the memory back to times that were and bring to mind a succession of details, that if they have disappeared, no that is why they cease to be less interesting for those who live by daily impressions.

Tango was born by accident: it was an eyesore and then it took suggestive and delusional forms.

Just as the Spanish airs have the ¡olé! of its vibrant nervousness, tango has the ¡ah, criollo! with which the teachers of the ravine are encouraged and applauded.

Let's make history!

The year was 1877 and in the "Mondongo" neighborhood, as the southern part of the municipality was called at that time, the headquarters of the candombés societies had been established, formed by men and women of color, whose origin dated back to the time of slavery.

There were some divisions between the most prestigious associates and, naturally, this gave rise to rancor and rivalries.

When the carnival date arrived, they would go out into the street with their outlandish, garish costumes and their enormous, feathered hats, dancing after long hours to the monotonous beat of candombés and masacayas.

The supremacy that each one tried to exercise, gave rise to furious rivalries and with it to bloody encounters in the middle of public roads.

The repetition of events brought as a consequence the dissolution of bellicose associations and the closure of their candombés.

Thus, drowning out the African expansions, dance centers were formed with the same elements, giving rise to the memorable tango little by little, but in a very different form from the one performed today.

The couples, instead of getting closer, separated to the beat, imitating the gesticulations and swaggers of the past candombé.

The new dance became general and shortly after it was spread, the compadritos from the suburbs took it for themselves and took it to the raw neighborhood of Los Corrals, where the "peringundines" were already operating with the traditional milonga.

The tango came to form a kind of currency, behind which those who cackled as skillful and brave in the handling of steel hid themselves.

Thus, the one who danced the best was the most "Taurus" and the most requested of the ladies.

The dance took root with such fury that the performers began to appear everywhere with different characteristics, but always under a plan of art and skill.

As in all new things, it did not take long to spread to other neighborhoods, moving to the academies that, shortly after, began to function in Barracas, Solís and Comercio, Solís and America, of bloody memory and finally in Pozos and Independencia, as perhaps the most famous for the bronze people who frequented it and for the prestige of the dancers who attended.

There they laid down their fame as super tangoists — as the Cavallieri says in Europe — "Refucilo, la parda", "Pepa, la chata", "Lola, la petisa", "La Mondonguito", "Maria la Vasca", "La China Venicia", "María la Tero" and others with original nicknames they had. the scepter of suburban preferences.

That academy, which was founded at the height of tango enthusiasm, brought together elements of different kinds, strengthening its popularity during the short period it lived.

The blackened halls were attended not only by breakdown people, but even by those who were called "packs" at that time, but who in the interpretation of tango were more skillful and masters in footwork.

Many with well-known surnames are still remembered who hold high positions in the national administration and even deputies and military officers who, with the self-esteem of good dancers, disputed the honor of victory in an interlude.

Indifferent to any criticism, they did not hesitate to rub elbows and even braid each other in an iron to iron fight with any quarrelsome compadrito.

These frequent scenes put Commissioner Villamayor of the 18th in serious conflict more than once, who, with the severity of his character, managed to put the "pesaos" of San Cristóbal at bay.

He established the requisition of weapons for each assistant, but as the prohibition squeezes the ingenuity, there were those who, displaying extreme skill, managed to sneak in without abandoning the fighting instrument.

The police chronicles came to deal frequently with the criollo duels that took place almost every night and this was the reason for the closure of such a dangerous meeting point.

For a "get those straws out of there", two favorites of any dancer, one of those Chinese of native ancestry, whose prank consisted of testing the courage of her gallants, came out to settle the matter.

At that time there was a true cult for the reckless and chivalrous value of the combatants, citing cases in which one of the duelists resisted going to the encounter, if his adversary was not on equal arms.

Regarding these events, an old police officer told us one day:

"Imagine, that one night, Pancho the heavyweight of the corrals came out challenged with another who also had the reputation of handsome and when he went out to the street he asked him:

— Do you have weapons? - To which the other replied: No, but it is! the same, because I'm going to punch you!

— Wait a minute, — he told him, — I'm coming. — Don't move from here — and he ran towards a hardware store that speaks in front of the academy.

In a few moments he returned finding his rival at the same point.

— Well, here you are to defend yourself, — he told him, handing her a 16-inch-long dagger. Then he added:

— Now get ready because I'm going to put a mask on your face, so you will remember me."

And in the darkness of the night, they intertwined in terrible combat. When we went to the police station, the two were lying on the ground, pierced by more than twenty stab wounds.

Such was the characteristic of those times, when the brave was respected and the bad hitters were condemned, when they attacked and wounded from behind.

The repudiation felt by an individual of such conditions was worse than a sentence of twenty years.

In the academy of Independencia and Pozos was where tango had its greatest heyday, adopting a cadenced and rhythmic system that does not exist today, because it has been modified enormously, losing the typical cachet that only the dances of that time knew how to imprint on it.

It is also true that the dancers of the past have disappeared and that the tango authors themselves -with the exception of Bevilacqua, Pérez Freire and Solá, for example- have mistaken the true harmony and composition of their origin.

The Negro Casimiro, who was the first to make his tangos known along with the mulatto Sinforoso — a clarinet that played alone from so many ginebrones —, was the one who produced the largest number of compositions of this nature, popularizing them even on the barrel organs.

The black composer became one of the best performers at the Academy, due to the tingling that he imparted to his old and patched-up violin.

Casimiro was a popular guy, currently being seen by the national distributions, playing Martin Pescador, with that good-natured and friendly character that characterized him.

There is no lack of old acquaintances who from time to time loosen a "five" for a liter, as he calls, ironically, his old hobbies of raising the elbow.

Before these Academies, the name given to them due to the modernization of tango, there were the famous Peringundines in remote neighborhoods and among them that of the corridors of the old Plaza de Lorea, where the fame of Carmen Gómez stood out, a skillful milonguera, capable of charging against a cavalry cadre.

This was the obligatory meeting point for the soldiers of an infantry battalion that at that time occupied the building on Calle Alsina y Lorea.

Not a night went by without the militia coming out at gunpoint with the "carreros" and "compadritos" who frequented the room.

This, when the dancing ladies did not think to end the party with cuts and stabs. As none of them dropped the "garbage spit", as soon as they felt bellicose impetus due to excess of the cane, they undertook it with a straight shot with the tertulians and cleared the room in less than five minutes.

This peringundin was closed shortly after due to the statistics of crimes that were recorded.

He is still remembered by many men who show off cords and gallons earned on the battlefields. Around the year 1880, after the revolution, tango resurfaced with greater force, going beyond the limits of the suburbs and implanting itself in the center of the city.

Despite the fact that dance houses were prohibited, some of them managed to establish themselves in the gloomy neighborhood of Corrientes, which, as is known, was the focus of the dens of vice.

They adopted the system of the little organ covered with a mattress, so that the echoes would not transcend the public road and reach the ears of the police authority, something unlikely because they knew it and consented to it.

The "Stella di Roma", Corrientes and Uruguay, known for "El baile de Pepín" (the ball of Pepín), was the first to establish itself and the one with the greatest boom due to the attraction exerted by the Balbina sisters, Rosa and María.

Later the "Scudo de Italia" emerged, where the Apollo theater now exists.

La Benevolenza in front of Roma, Provin's house; the Puentecito and others that had an ephemeral life, because after a certain time the police finished with them, but not before their owners became rich.

In this neighborhood, tango underwent great innovations, changing not only its figures, but also its elasticity and sway, which was the interesting characteristic of its origin.

Performed by mostly Italian girls, they did not adapt to the movement that the criollos of stock imprinted on it and it was then that it was given the name "tango liso" (flat tango).

The modification became almost general, losing the primitive air.

For this reason, many of those who danced there failed in the Academies.

However, famous fans like skinny Saúl, for example, identified with both styles and danced with equal ease in one or the other hall.

Mariano the dancer, a regular attendee at the Scudo in Italy, where a Paulina had the entire clientele upset, was another of those who exercised the scepter of popularity, due to the correctness with which he performed.

Tango lovers made a wheel for him every time he occupied the dance floor, to admire and applaud him in the difficult execution of figures that he invented and that no one else could imitate.

Those dancers who were, are today householders and parents who honestly defend their interests as landowner and merchant, respectively.

The latter owns an important commercial establishment on Calle de Sarmiento at the height of Carlos Pellegrini.

Tango continued to develop enthusiastically until the Politeama and Skating Rink companies (today San Martín), took it to their rooms as a new exponent for the general public.

It is useless to add that it was a complete success.

The reign of the dance lasted two years, after which it disappeared and with it the male and female dancers also disappeared, many of whom were scattered throughout La Plata and towns in the province, where the Academies made an appearance.

They also had a sad end there.

In the district of Tolosa, in the provincial capital, some of them were installed in the "La alpargatería", because it was founded by a Basque espadrille maker, but as bloody scenes occurred, the police agreed with the municipality and proceeded to its closure.

This is the true story of the dance that has just resurfaced in public life, adorning itself with tinsel of confetti to cross the Atlantic, prevail abroad and then return to the homeland with purple cloaks and cardboard laurels.

Tango has been talked about so much, it has been praised so much, that we have been forced to deal with the subject extensively, pointing out its evolution and presenting it with naked clothing so that the public knows what its origins are and who inspired it.

The tango is, in fact, gently undulating, with a measured and daring rhythm, but it has the drawback of not having been well understood by those who intend to bring it back to life.

In the style of all danceable pieces, it has its measure and beat, within which the performers must adjust the special sway that the music marks.

The flex is one of the most culminating details.

If the dancer does not print this cadence, within a real time, the piece lacks interest. If the dancer, for example, does not know how to perform double footwork backwards, she cannot be a good performer.

Tango is not danced at will and rigidly.

We have been able to notice that a large part of the dancers is moving away from the beat, interposing movements that conflict with the beat and harmony.

The step forward, the sitting on the tip of the right foot and the tapping, must be done according to the marked times.

In a word, each figure must end with the musical beat.

If these rules are forgotten, the artistic value is lost and declines.

The position of the dancer with his partner and the way of taking the arm, is another important detail for a good execution.

We'll see if these details are met in tonight's contest at the Palace Theater.

For our part, we intend to make a detailed criticism on the matter, since tango has reached the heights and it is about imposing itself in aristocratic circles.

Tonight, then, the old tango that came to national life with a shameful stigma, resurfaces like Gounod's old Fausto on the aristocratic stage to make its triumphal entrance as a well-to-do child, dressed up in the prim clothing of the impeccable tailcoat and gentle gloved hands. »

In 1913, the Uruguayan musician Alberico Spatola (1885 – 1941) made his debut as professional player at the Parisién café on 300 Esmeralda Street, Buenos Aires, when he played as trumpeter of a ballroom orchestra.

The trumpet was his first instrument and later, the piano.

Back in 1909 he composed a tango, "La sucursal", with which he won the first prize at a contest of the Teatro Avenida.

On that occasion of his debut, he composed his most well-known number, the tango "El 13" (The Thirteen), symbol of the year of its creation (1913).

Ángel Villoldo wrote its lyrics.

They repeated the collaboration in 1914 with the tango "El 14" (Petit Duc).

In 1914 he put together his own tango orchestra with which he appeared at the carnival balls of the "Teatro Coliseo" in Buenos Aires

The lyrics of the tangos "El 13" and "El 14" are the nirvana of the quest for the tango that all "tangueros" and tangoists dream of achieving.

They are the true apologia to the feeling of tango-dance, the Tangasm.

Tango "El 13/El Trece" (The 13/The Thirteen), 1913

How lovely it is to dance
A sleepy tango,
To enjoy, to dream, to live,
To feel the vibrations of the heart!

When with sorrow
I sway to the beat,
I do not know what happens to me,
I feel a joy like no other.

When I'm spellbound in the arms of my lovely woman
My heart is full of passion and pleasure
And the sweet swing of the dance makes me really happy
And it is the voluptuous "El Trece", and I love it.

It is a tango for dancing
A very unique dance
That enraptures the soul
And fills us with emotions.

Tango is my great passion
And my heart beats
When I dance with a Creole
A nice leg, and my heart is moved.
https://youtu.be/Z_uEzQ-IHao

* * * * *
Tango "El 14" (Petit Duc), 1914

What a unique joy
and what an emotion
you feel dancing a tango,
when the one who dances is a leg
and with the hot
we sway to the beat.
We feel throughout the body,
nonstop
a voluptuous dizziness;
with the sway
it gives me a tingle
that cannot be explained.

Tango is a divine thing
if you dance with passion.

Fill our soul with joy
and floods us with love.

When my Creole takes me
What a pleasure to make the little dip!
My whole being is moved,
with ardor,
in the arms of my sweetheart.
And when making the "media luna",
no need to talk,
they get excited.

We are acclaimed
as the most famous
in the art of "compadriar".

This compliment is top notch
and not everyone does.

This "corte" compadrón
it's only for who
knows how to do it very well.
https://youtu.be/RfJgKZPZp1Y

In 1915, Angel Villoldo published the lyrics of the tangos "El 13" and "El 14" among songs of deep national contents titled "Cantos Populares Argentinos" (Argentine Popular Songs) for the purpose of commemorating of the centennial of the declaration of the Independence:
https://digital.iai.spk-berlin.de/viewer/image/83597863X/18/
https://digital.iai.spk-berlin.de/viewer/image/83597863X/19/
https://digital.iai.spk-berlin.de/viewer/image/83597863X/20/

"From the Café, the tango passed to Europe, and is due to recognize that during the "little trip" it became aristocratized, managing to open the doors of all the ballrooms, from where it left when it wanted, and finally taking refuge in the cabaret." ~ Angel Villoldo
https://youtu.be/9qhWqepQcbo

LOS BAILES DE MI PAGO

EL mulato Arroyo, antiguo sargento del regimiento de Blandengues, está de fiesta; su rancho, el más blanqueadito de las orillas, ha sufrido las transformaciones del caso: el dormitorio será la sala de baile, para lo cual la vieja cama de fierro se ha trasladado á un obscuro rincón de la pieza vecina, donde apenas se distinguen los colores de la colcha de percal floreado.

Sobre una rinconera, más cerca del techo que del piso, arde la lámpara, cuyo reflector proyecta la luz sobre dos oleografías de tintas chillonas que en un tiempo fueron *réclame* de un fabricante de licores; alineadas á lo largo del muro están las sillas, altas unas, bajas otras, pocas con el respaldo entero y todas con las patas temblorosas.

dos se confunden, y la bailarina con la cabeza reclinada sobre el hombro de su compañero, baila, completamente entregada á éste, que gira ya á la derecha, ya á la izquierda, aprovechando las pausas rafadas de la música, para hacer un cortecito y estrechar contra su pecho el seno palpitante de la criolla.

La fiesta continúa sin interrupción, mientras varios paisanos arrimados á la única ventana observan y critican:

—¿Te fijastes, Simón, cómo se hamacaba la gorda?

—¡Callate, hermano! Sí el que tiene que hamacarse es Pepe, porque ella es más pesada que un arau de cuatro rejas!...

—¡Oiga, doña Juana!...

—¿Qué dice, don Simón? ¿qué hace que no dentra?

Del piso, previamente regado, se levanta un vaho húmedo, impregnado del suave olor á tierra mojada.

Los músicos han llegado, precedidos del meritorio de la policía y del confitero de la esquina de la plaza, que son los dueños del baile; aquél paga la música y éste pone yerba, masas y ginebra. Ellos son los que invitan, y á ellos se dirigen los que de paso solicitan autorización para echar una piernita.

El baile comienza; las dos guitarras dejan oir las primeras notas de una pieza y un acompañamiento; las mozas entran, sonriendo á los convidados, que bajo el alero del rancho esperan una habanera que se preludia.

Suena al fin, voluptuosa y lasciva, con ritmos y cadencias que sólo conoce el guitarrero del campo; todos se empujan por llegar primero y el baile se arma: las parejas se abrazan estrechamente, las piernas se rozan sin que el pudor se resienta, los alientos caldea-

—No; si ya me voy. Quería preguntarle si hay alguna laguna cerca...

—Vaya, pues; ¡hágase el nuevo en el pago! ¿No sabe que no hay ninguna?

—¿Y entonces, patrona, de ande ha podido sacar tanto bagre?

Un coro de carcajadas estalla, celebrando la guasada del paisano; las lindas se sonríen, las feas se quedan serias, Doña Juana continúa circulando la bandeja de masas y las copas de licor de menta, mientras algunas viejas, después de un «¡vaya con el hombre!» siguen, entre mate y mate, cabeceando en los rincones, y los guitarreros, trás de un buen taco de ginebra, rasguean una mazurca llorona.

MATACO.

Dib. de Fortuny.

Figure 7: "Tango Criollo" – magazine Caras y Caretas, Year II, no. 16, page 9, Buenos Aires, Argentina, 1899 January 21

5 THE TANGO QUINTESSENCE

The Tangomania of 1913 was responsible for planting a seed under the development of the most important cosmopolitan cities in the world. Although the Tango seed of "La Vie Heureuse" ("The Happy Life") faded after the First World War and was almost lost after the Second World War. But it will always sprout again and again even on scorched earth with the blessing of the Goddess Terpsichore.

Although it is not extinct, tango kept its secret in places outside the world of new avant-garde tango, and some artists brought out songs about the lost essence of the Tangomania in 1913, as is the case with these five American and French popular songs:

I. Song "I Get Ideas", Eileen Wilson, 1951
II. Song "Takes Two To Tango", Pearl Bailey, 1957
III. Song "Sway", Rosemary Clooney, 1959
IV. Song "Invitango", Brigitte Bardot 1963
V. Song "Paris un Tango", Mireille Mathieu, 1971

I. Song "I Get Ideas", Eileen Wilson, 1951

The music of "I Get Ideas" is a 1927 tango-song called "Adiós Muchachos" composed by the Argentinian Julio Cesar Sanders (often credited in the United States as "Lenny Sanders"). The lyrics in English (which have nothing to do with the original Argentine lyrics by Cesar Felipe Vedani) are by Dorcas Cochran and were published in 1951. The video shows a lesson of tango de salon, in which Eileen Wilson sings in 1951: https://youtu.be/o9RArPxP9Y0

"I Get Ideas", 1951

When we are dancing and your dangerously near me
I get ideas, I get ideas
I want to hold you so much closer than I dare to
I want to scold you 'cause I care more than I care to
And when you touch me and there's fire in every finger
I get ideas, I get ideas

And after we have kissed goodnight and still you linger
I kinda think you get ideas too
Your eyes are always saying
The things you're never saying
I only hope they're saying that you could love me too
For that's the whole idea, it's true
The lovely idea that I'm falling in love with you

When we are dancing and your dangerously near me
I get ideas, I get ideas
I want to hold you so much closer than I dare to
I want to scold you 'cause I care more than I care to

And when you touch me and there's fire in every finger
I get ideas, I get ideas
And after we have kissed goodnight and still you linger
I kinda think you get ideas too

Your eyes are always saying
The things you're never saying
I only hope they're saying that you could love me too
For that's the whole idea, it's true
The lovely idea that I'm falling in love with you

II. Song "Takes Two To Tango", Pearl Bailey, 1957

"Takes Two To Tango" is a popular song, written by Al Hoffman and Dick Manning and published in 1952. The lyrics are remarkable and the video from the Nat King Cole Show and Pearl Bailey in 1957 shows many of the steps of Tangomania era:
https://youtu.be/vDc9re0clzc

"Takes Two To Tango", 1952

You can haunt any house by yourself
Be a man or a mouse by yourself
You can act like a king on a throne
There are lots of things that you can do alone
But it takes...

Two to tango, two to tango
Two to really get the feeling of romance
Two to tango, two to tango
Do the dance of love

You can sail on a ship by yourself
Take a nap or a nip by yourself
You can get into bed on your own
There are lots of things that you can do alone
I said....

Two to tango, two to tango
Two to really get the feeling of romance
Two to tango, two to tango
Do the dance of love

You can get buried all by yourself
Catch a fish or a cold by yourself
Dig a ditch, strike it rich all by yourself
There are lots of things that you can do alone
But it takes...

Two to tango, two to tango
Two to really get the feeling of romance
Two to tango, two to tango
Do the dance of love

You can fight like a champ by yourself
You can lick any stamp by yourself
You can be very brave on the phone
There are lots of things that you can do alone
I said it takes...

Two to tango, two to tango
Two to really get the feeling of romance
Two to tango, two to tango
Do the dance of love

It takes two, I said two
Darling it always takes two,
I'm with you!

III. Song "Sway", Rosemary Clooney, 1959

In 1954, the English lyrics of "Sway" ("Quien Será") was written by Norman Gimbel and recorded by Dean Martin backed by Dick Stabile's orchestra. In this video Rita Hayworth is dancing Spanish Tango with Anthony Quinn in the movie Blood and Sand (1941), and Rosemary Clooney is singing Sway in 1959:
https://youtu.be/P5Dx0pQ4BVY

"Sway", 1954

When marimba rhythms start to play
Dance with me, make me sway
Like a lazy ocean hugs the shore
Hold me close, sway me more

Like a flower petal in the breeze
Bend with me, sway with ease
When we dance you have a way with me
Stay with me, sway with me

Other dancers may be on the floor
Dear, but my eyes will see only you
Only you have the magic technique
When we sway I go weak

I can hear the sound of violins
Long before it begins
Make me thrill as only you know how
Sway me smooth, sway me now

Other dancers may be on the floor
Dear, but my eyes will see only you
Only you have the magic technique
When we sway I go weak

I can hear the sound of violins
Long before it begins
Make me thrill as only you know how
Sway me smooth, sway me now
You know how
Sway me smooth, sway me now

IV. Song "Invitango", Brigitte Bardot, 1963

In 1963, the famous French actress Brigitte Bardot launch a musical album with a remarkable song inviting the memories of the Tangomania era in Paris in 1913:
https://youtu.be/meJHldwp9C8

"Invitango", 1963

I invite you to the indecency
of this nearly Argentine tango
where I will be acquainted
with your body against mine;

where you will discover
this exotic conversation.
When music is offered,
know it: it must be followed.

(chorus)
Step into my tango
and I will dance you
with half closed lids.
Lost, among reflections
of the music that carries us away ...
As the violins
tell about their sorrow.

Our fingers intertwined
as the petals of a flower
will convince you that I am yours
and you are close to my heart ...

I will tell you in Spanish
the loving words I know
and we will see who loses his head
first under the influence of...

(chorus)
Step into my tango
and I will dance you
with half closed lids.
Lost, among reflections

of the music that carries us away ...
As the violins
tell about their sorrow.

I say "tu"(you) to you, we are old enough
to say "tu"(you) to each other even if we're not acquainted.
And since the tango compels you
to recognize me forever...
We might as well not fuss about it
and start kissing each other
since they dimmed the lights
to spare us the embarrassment ...

Step into my love,
I will "Argentinize" you
till dawn breaks
To show you the country you like.
The tango alone is to blame...
for this beautiful, unforgettable trip.

They ask weird questions;
don't even listen to them.
They would do anything
to make me miss my step...
From this sexy rhythm,
what will remain?
I know where the tango begins,
where will it end in this tale ...
of this nearly Argentine tango?

I invite you to indecency.

V. Song "Paris un Tango", Mireille Mathieu, 1971

In 1971, the famous French singer Mireille Mathieu song a theme "Paris un Tango" often performed in German "Pariser Tango" that clearly evokes the memories of the Tangomania era in Paris in 1913:
https://youtu.be/jFSRfT5eje8

"Paris, a Tango", 1971

This is the true tango of the old days.
This is the true Paris — listen to me.
Here, you only have to draw out a few steps.
There, it's coming back to you already.

Tango, Paris, a tango — all the better, bravo, thank you, my tango.
Thank you for giving us your nights in music and in the oblivion
of another tango — my life, a tango — all the better, bravo for your dance.
You can leave us in the morning, tango, but come back to us tomorrow.

Every night in a cafe on a street in my neighborhood,
an old accordionist plays his songs to tourists.
But a melody, always the same, a tango serves as a refrain
to lovers who come like the both of us to sing to him.

This is the true tango of the old days.
This is the true Paris — listen to me.
Here, you only have to draw out a few steps.
There, it's coming back to you already.

Tango, Paris, a tango — all the better, bravo, thank you, my tango.
Thank you for returning suddenly and for having all the steps
during a tango — my life, a tango — all the better, bravo for your dance.
You can leave us in the morning but, tango, come back to us tomorrow.

You can leave us in the morning, tango, now I will hold onto you!

(Paris, a tango — my life, a tango.)

Figure 8: "Parfum Tango", an Ad for Tango perfume, by Gabilla
perfumeries, magazine Femina, Paris, 1914 February 15

«I had never danced the tango, but an Argentine boy who served as my guide insisted with me to try it. With my first timid steps I felt my pulse responding to the incessant languid rhythm of that voluptuous dance, soft as a long caress, intoxicating as love in the midday sun, cruel and dangerous as the seduction of a tropical forest.» ~ Isadora Duncan, when she visited Buenos Aires in 1916
https://youtu.be/-eQhocYRhoI

Figure 9: "A Tango Tea House", cover of the magazine Life, New York, 1914 April 9.

IMAGES CREDITS

Figure 1: Le Tango de la Coupé, 1913
https://www.parismuseescollections.paris.fr/fr/musee-carnavalet/oeuvres/album-tangoville-sur-mer-le-tango-de-la-coupe
https://www.sem-goursat.com/album19

Figure 2: Tango de Salón, 1913
https://hprints.com/en/item/70328/?u=1,2
https://youtu.be/9678HgImENg

Figure 3: Tango Tee, 1914
https://babel.hathitrust.org/cgi/pt?id=mdp.39015021037992&view=1up&seq=205&skin=2021
https://youtu.be/6M8BWVHO83k

Figure 4: Le Tango, 1913
https://hprints.com/en/item/76855/?u=1,6
https://gallica.bnf.fr/ark:/12148/btv1b6927888p

Figure 5: Tango Habanera, 1858
https://gallica.bnf.fr/ark:/12148/btv1b525038298/f1.item
https://gallica.bnf.fr/ark:/12148/bpt6k857977m/f1.item

Figure 6: La Leçon de Tango, 1913
https://hprints.com/en/item/85377/
https://youtu.be/wEmGtzPNo8s

Figure 7: Tango Criollo, 1899
http://hemerotecadigital.bne.es/issue.vm?id=0004082343&page=9
http://hemerotecadigital.bne.es/issue.vm?id=0004081262&page=10

Figure 8: Parfum Tango, 1914
https://hprints.com/en/item/80706/?u=1,1
https://gallica.bnf.fr/ark:/12148/bpt6k6556563w/f54.item

Figure 9: A Tango Tea House, 1914
https://babel.hathitrust.org/cgi/pt?id=mdp.39015033933485&view=1up&seq=639&skin=2021
https://www.academia.edu/47756964/The_Arrival_of_Tango_in_Japan_Allure_Fear_and_Morality_in_Early_20_th_Century_Japan_1_Yuiko_Asaba

Figure 10: Exit Tango, 1916
https://www.prints-online.com/south-america-tango-longer-fashionable-14393981.html
https://youtu.be/0NHjYCqaoTk

Figure 11: La Veuve Joyeuse, 1923
https://www.parismuseescollections.paris.fr/fr/musee-carnavalet/oeuvres/album-le-nouveau-monde-2eme-serie-la-veuve-joyeuse-0
https://www.sem-goursat.com/album25

Que peuvent-ils faire sans Tango?
What can they do without the Tango?   AMÉRIQUE DU SUD

Figure 10: "Exit Tango", South America - The tango is no longer fashionable. A musician specializing in the music of the tango returns home from Europe once the craze for this particular style has passed, 1916

ABOUT THE AUTHOR

Augusto Tomas is one of thousands worldwide aficionados of the Tango. His life is a Tango whose life modeled him to become an exquisite "Professeur de Tango".

He learned from zero to hero the secrets behind the tango dance since it was announced to the world in the year of the Tangomania of 1913.

He danced the Tango all over the world and he has found that the seeds from the era of the Tangomania are still alive on the memories of the humankind.

Augusto Tomas is a member of the Le Conseil International de la Danse (CID-UNESCO).

https://www.facebook.com/tangoterroir

https://www.facebook.com/tangochampan

https://www.instagram.com/slow.tango.algarve/

Figure 11: Album Le Nouveau Monde (2ème série) : La Veuve Joyeuse, 1923, illustration by Sem (aka Georges Goursat)

Printed in Great Britain
by Amazon